The Way We Were?

The Way We Were?

The Myths and Realities of America's Student Achievement

Richard Rothstein

A Century Foundation Report

formerly the Twentieth Century Fund

1998 • The Century Foundation Press • New York

The Century Foundation, formerly the Twentieth Century Fund, sponsors and supervises timely analyses of economic policy, foreign affairs, and domestic political issues. Not-for-profit and nonpartisan, it was founded in 1919 and endowed by Edward A. Filene.

Cataloging in Publication Data

Rothstein, Richard.
The way we were? : the myths and realities of America's student achievement / Richard Rothstein.
p. cm. -- (A Century Foundation report)
Includes bibliographical references (p.) and index.
ISBN 0-87078-417-X
1. Education--United States. 2. Academic achievement--United States.
3. Children of minorities--Education--United States.
I. Title. II. Series
LA210.R63 1998 98-34018
371.01'0973--DC21 CIP

Cover design and illustration: Claude Goodwin
Cover photo: Lang Photo, Virginia
Manufactured in the United States of America.

FOREWORD

An extensive recent survey suggested that, despite a decline in reported crime, most Americans believed that crime was continuing to increase. At the same time, the researchers found that more and more television news time was devoted to stories about crime. While the relationship between these findings is only suggestive, the possibility that the facts about crime were lost in the perceptions fostered by coverage may be significant.

In a sense, in the pages that follow, Richard Rothstein makes a similar argument about public education—but one with even more force. He presents important evidence that the nation's public schools are performing as well as or better than ever (and even that most parents are happy with their children's schools), yet the public debate about education is largely framed in terms of failure and decline. Such public lamentation, in fact, has been heard about American education for generations. If one collected the typical comments made about public education in the United States over the course of the past century, and knew nothing else about U.S. history, one could quite logically conclude that the nation must have failed dismally in its attempts to become part of the modern world.

Recent criticism has taken two forms: the first emphasizes the shortcomings of urban public schools, especially in poor neighborhoods, and the second stresses "declines" in scores on Scholastic Assessment Tests (SATs). Both are combined with ample anecdotal evidence of teacher incompetence, administrative resistance to change, and districtwide financial mismanagement. But do such cases prove much more than that any system employing about 3.5 million human beings is sure to have a fair number of incompetents and bad apples? The answer to this question, as you might expect, depends not just upon whom you ask but also on what data and anecdotes you choose to believe.

Rothstein has sifted the information carefully, with a wary eye for the dangers of too glib a reading of this tea leaf or that. He is well aware of the difficulty of gathering data about educational achievement, particularly when measuring student performance over time. He provides an overview of the statistical methods currently in use, detailing their strengths and weaknesses. He cautions, for example, against simply comparing the SAT scores of a small self-selected group of largely upper-class, Ivy League-bound students—who comprised the great majority of test takers in the early postwar years—to those of the current, much more broadly based set of test takers from very diverse socioeconomic groups.

Rothstein also offers insights into some of the hot topics in education such as social promotion, the teaching of phonics, and the continuing debate about bilingual education, controversies that have been around for a long time. Although many critics of today's educational establishment yearn for some past golden age and call for a return to basics, there is no hard evidence to support their belief that the past was golden and no proof that current practices are harmful. Indeed, the various adaptations in educational practice over the years are a reflection of pragmatic adaptations by schools to the conditions of their time and place and to the demands of parents and teachers. The critics of modern teaching methods ignore the progress that has been made in this area while providing few ideas about how minority achievement could be enhanced. In sum, Rothstein constructs an impressive argument for his conclusion that schools are providing our children with increasingly good educations. He believes that, rather than radical reform, we need steady, consistent, and historically informed critiques of what we are doing married to a program of gradual change.

The Century Foundation is the new name of the Twentieth Century Fund, an institution that has examined many aspects of American education, in such works as Warren Bennis's *The Leaning Ivory Tower; Making the Grade*, the report of the Twentieth Century Fund Task Force on Federal Elementary and Secondary Education Policy;

and *Hard Lessons: Public Schools and Privatization* by Carol Ascher, Norm Fruchter, and Robert Berne. With this report, Richard Rothstein continues our tradition of looking with fresh eyes at public issues. On behalf of our Trustees, I thank him for this effort.

RICHARD C. LEONE, *PRESIDENT*
The Century Foundation
August 1998

Contents

ACKNOWLEDGMENTS

Were it not for Gerald Bracey's tilting at windmills, a suffocating consensus about declining student achievement might have prevented even the contemplation of a report like this. Americans seeking reasoned discussion of public school accomplishments and problems may disagree with his approach, but nonetheless they owe him a debt of gratitude for making debate possible. David Berliner and Bruce Biddle, Harold Hodgkinson, and Iris Rotberg have also helped bring balance to our public school debates. Followers of their writings will not be surprised by findings here.

As the notes reveal, this report was particularly influenced by several scholars who examine data about student achievement without ideological preconceptions. I wish to thank them specifically, beyond the text's formal citations of their work. They include David Grissmer, H. D. Hoover, and Daniel Koretz. H. D. not only led by example but generously opened his files to me. The text has no specific citations to Christopher Jencks, but his approach to data in social policy—understanding that finding an unambiguous number is not the same as finding an unambiguous answer—has been an important influence. Discussions with Martin Orland, associate commissioner of education statistics at the U.S. Department of Education, helped to focus my questions and avoid overenthusiastic interpretations.

I am grateful to two colleagues upon whom I frequently rely for advice, counsel, and correction; they not only provided these but read the manuscript and guided its final revisions—Professor James Guthrie of Vanderbilt University and Nancy Protheroe, research director of the Educational Research Service. Larry Mishel, my research director at the Economic Policy Institute, is my ultimate superego for whatever intellectual work I attempt.

The idea for this report came from Robert Kuttner, coeditor of *The American Prospect*, and he pursued it with Century Foundation president Richard Leone. It would not have happened without each of them. I am particularly grateful to Leone, who stuck with this project even when its themes appeared counterintuitive to many of his advisers. The report took me too long to finish, but I was prodded by insightful education reporters Mike Rose and Peter Schrag, and by William Fowler at NCES, each of whom nagged me to return to it when other commitments competed.

The historical research for this report was conducted at the Occidental College library, where John de la Fontaine, director of the library's document delivery service, went out of his way to be helpful. Student research assistants Erik Rasmussen, Linh Thai, and Jen Uyeda did the legwork to track down the sources. Tyler Carter and Debbie Shupack searched out ancient newspaper clippings in other states.

A series of Century Foundation editors—Beverly Goldberg, Michelle Miller, Jon Shure, David Smith, and Ken Emerson—stuck with this project as I procrastinated in completing it. I thank them for their patience. Copy editor Steven Greenfield demonstrated that even I can be outnitpicked, and the text is very much the better for it.

Five years as a budget program analyst for the Los Angeles School Board, under the thoughtful tutelage of Roger Rasmussen, gave me a better feel for public education data than I otherwise could have obtained. My wife, Judith, the principal of an inner-city middle school, regales me daily with anecdotes that put life into these data while insulating them from too-glib interpretation. Jesse, Leah, and Amy got much better educations in their middle-class public schools in the 1980s and 1990s than I received forty years ago—and mine was, in some respects, pretty good. This reality, above all, provided an insight underlying the themes of this report. With gratitude, this report is dedicated to their teachers.

Introduction

The dilemma of how to improve our public schools perplexes many Americans. There is a widely shared—though by no means unanimous—consensus about four propositions:

1. American student achievement has declined in the past generation, and public school standards have deteriorated. Graduates know less now than they used to.

2. The crisis is especially severe for urban minority youth, who attend schools that no longer provide an engine of mobility for those at the bottom of the socioeconomic ladder. On the contrary, predominantly minority schools are now so inferior that they actively hold young people back from achieving their potential.

3. Even if academic achievement has not deteriorated to the extent widely believed, our schools do not produce graduates with skills necessary for the emerging, twenty-first-century economy.

4. American educational failure is confirmed by the poor performance of our students on international tests. Young Americans cannot compete with youths in other nations.

The pages that follow show that these claims are similar, indeed nearly identical, to what has been said about American schools for a century or more. In each generation the claims proved false. Having been wrong before does not necessarily mean the conventional wisdom is wrong today, but awareness of this history should make people more cautious about jumping again to the same conclusions. When propositions are disproved repeatedly, those who advance them yet another time should bear a heavy burden of proof.

This report goes on to show that contemporary claims of school failure do not meet such a serious burden of proof. In part the claims are just plain wrong, and in part there is simply no credible evidence or adequate data with which to evaluate them. Without such evidence, assertions of school inadequacy are generally supported by selective invocation of anecdotes. Certainly, a nuanced analysis of American education must rely on anecdotes as well as hard statistics. But in the absence of data, anecdotes should be treated with skepticism, especially when they are used to support a viewpoint with a long history of inaccuracy and exaggeration.

It would be easy for critics to caricature this report by claiming it seeks no improvements in American education. This would be unfair. Institutions, our public schools serving as no exception, should always be criticized, examined, and improved. Reformers have an important role in exposing flaws in and proposing solutions for even the best of them. Many anecdotes used to illustrate school failure are true; though they may not prove the themes for which they are intended, they are useful in directing attention to areas where improvement is not only possible but also necessary.

Of the four widespread suppositions about public schools—declining achievement, betrayal of minority aspirations, inadequate workforce skills, and relative international failure—this short report critiques only the first two in detail. A concluding chapter briefly discusses why a more extensive examination might show the other two to be equally wrongheaded.

The report's first chapter summarizes commonplace indictments of our public schools and shows that contemporary criticisms are little different from those made generations before. In itself, this does not invalidate them. But because they are often presented as though based on recent developments, audiences should be more skeptical of such critiques than they might otherwise be.

Chapter 2 suggests that, in a nation as large and complex as ours, anecdotal evidence can too easily be misleading. Even the most sophisticated understanding of broad trends in American education will, by summarizing the anecdotes, inevitably gloss over many cases that are far worse—and many that are far better—than the trends suggest. But too often, attempts to summarize schools' diversity of experience become preconceptions that prevent fair assessment of the weight of the evidence. Once such preconceptions are developed, there is an inevitable tendency to filter out anecdotes that do not support them. This has characterized Americans' understanding of their schools.

Overreliance on school anecdotes happens because good statistical data are hard to come by. This is not for lack of trying to assess schools. In truth, Americans have been obsessed with test results for generations and collect considerable data on student achievement. However, measurement of student achievement is complex—too complex for the social science methods presently available. This may seem difficult to believe for a nation as advanced as ours, but measuring student achievement is as difficult as any technological undertaking could be.

These measurement and evaluation problems were recently highlighted in a widely publicized study by *Education Week* and the Pew Charitable Trusts on the "urban challenge" in public education, published as final revisions were being made to this report. *Education Week* focused on the Cleveland schools, where only 15 percent of the district's fourth and ninth graders passed the 1997 state proficiency tests, as a "study in crisis":

> Many come to school too hungry, tired, or sick to learn. Largely because of housing problems, 20 percent change addresses every year. . . . Half the city's children live with only one parent, while 40 percent of its adult residents lack high school diplomas. Many students are raised by single parents who lack the time or know-how to visit schools, help with homework. . . .[1]

Surely, one wants to think, even with these serious problems, Cleveland schools can do better than a 15 percent proficiency rate; some urban districts with apparently similar problems *do* have better results. But how much better should be expected? For some observers, the answer is all too clear. The *New York Times* announced the *Education Week* report with a headline "Report Shows Urban Pupils Fall Far Short in Basic Skills." The *Times* article noted that in New York State, 39 percent of urban fourth graders had "basic" reading skills compared to 70 percent for nonurban fourth graders—to which New York's education commissioner reacted, "This is an unacceptable result and we are not going to let it stand."[2]

Is anything short of equal outcomes unacceptable? Are equal outcomes within reach? No matter how much schools improve, it is fantasy to expect classrooms whose students have parents that did not graduate from high school to achieve the same fourth grade reading scores as those classrooms where the parents are college graduates. No doubt many readers of this book who were fortunate enough to have college educations never expected it was the job of their children's schools to get them ready to read. I considered that was *my* job: "touch and feel" books were among my children's first playthings. But at Paul Revere School in Cleveland, according to kindergarten teacher Robin Fluke, "I have children in my class who have never seen toys before. They don't even recognize their name[s]."[3] If the test scores at Paul Revere are lower than the scores at the elementary school my children attended, does this mean Paul Revere is a worse school and Robin Fluke a worse teacher? Not necessarily, but an observer really cannot make that judgment because there is so little understanding of how much lower one should expect Revere's scores to be than scores in a middle-class school, considering Revere's more serious social problems. Some critics of American education assume that if only Ms. Fluke and her colleagues would drill their children in phonics and other "basics," Revere students would catch up with their more advantaged peers. This assumption seems implausible, but there are no good data by which its critics could be proved right or wrong.

At the beginning of the school year, Ms. Fluke sent home a letter asking for parent volunteers to help in her classroom. Only one parent responded. If Americans decide that academic achievement at urban schools like Paul Revere is so low that these schools ought to be deemed failures, perhaps new investment in school social workers (who could focus on tightening the connection between the school, parents, and social service agencies) could have a big payoff in test scores. But one of the most frequent criticisms of our urban schools is that they already spend too much money outside the classroom. Most people assume that this means a lot of bureaucracy, but in fact most urban school systems spend relatively little on bureaucracy; the big nonclassroom expenditures are often attempts to compensate for students' social problems. If Ms. Fluke's school were to invest in social workers, it would increase the percentage of Cleveland's funds spent outside the classroom and would subject the district to further criticism for that reason.

A child's educational achievement springs not only from the quality of schooling but also from health, motivational, family, and cultural conditions—many of which are set in the earliest years of life—for which schools are not responsible. Many Americans today believe that well-designed schools can make up for prior deficiencies in children's ability to learn, so that, by the end of schooling, all children can be held to the same high academic standards. This expectation is unlikely to prove practical, although the alternative—specification of different standards for children from different backgrounds—is fraught with moral and political dangers.

Even so, one certainly cannot evaluate school quality without sophisticated measures of how much value schools add to the raw material, the initial pupil characteristics, that schools inherit from families and communities. Surely, if society wants all children to read by fourth grade, a school deserves no plaudits for achieving this with a student body composed of children prepared to read as toddlers at home. A school with no such children might be a better school, even if it failed the read-by-fourth-grade standard. Chapter 3 discusses how little is known about the relationship between students' family characteristics and their learning, and how difficult it is to gather data by which the "value added" in schools can be measured.

In past generations, supporters of public schools were on the defensive, much as they are today. Chapter 3 also describes the counterattack most often employed by these defenders: "then and now" exercises in which school administrators or researchers readministered an ancient test to contemporary students, almost always showing that the contemporaries outperformed previous generations. Today, however, people have become too sophisticated about the limitations of both standardized tests and sampling procedures to grant credibility to a "then and now" exercise. This sophistication, however, has left public education with no easily mounted defense against irresponsible attacks.

Chapter 4 looks at three tests that now provide trend data on student achievement: the College Board's Scholastic Assessment Test (SAT), the Iowa Test of Basic Skills (ITBS), and the National Assessment of Educational Progress (NAEP).* Actual data, limited

---

* This book does not discuss two other tests. The ACT (American College Testing Program), used by some colleges and states, is a less publicized alternative to the SAT. ACT trends are even more difficult to analyze than SAT trends because of data limitations. The ITBS tests elementary school students. A companion test, the Iowa Test of Educational Development (ITED), assesses secondary students. The book does not deal with the ITED, although analysis of the ITED confirms the broad trends discussed in Chapter 4.

though they are, do not confirm the widespread view that achievement is declining. Even when SAT scores seem to decline, they mask a more complex, more positive picture. Chapter 4 concludes with a look at IQs, finding that, while not strictly an achievement measure, IQ trends may confirm a more encouraging interpretation of American student progress.

Chapter 5 looks particularly at test score patterns of minority students. While data here are sparse, trends give reason for hope, in marked distinction to a prevailing impression of educational disaster. There is still tremendous room, and need, for improvement. But if the signs are positive, it is likely that the best way to improve things is to continue approaches that thus far have been shown to be successful. This is one area where selective use of anecdotes and data can be particularly harmful to prospects for further gains.

It must be emphasized again that even if public schools have been performing well, this does not mean renewal and improvement should be neglected. But to embark upon treatment with inaccurate diagnoses is to make it more likely that the wrong medicine would be administered. Chapter 6 examines three of the most frequently advocated reforms designed to stiffen American educational standards: a "return" to phonics, an end to social promotion, and the abolition of bilingual education. "Back to basics" advocates generally take for granted that phonics, retention in grade, and English immersion were tried-and-true methods that once worked in American education but were abandoned in recent generations' relaxation of standards. Chapter 6 shows that, on the contrary, so-called traditional approaches were abandoned from 75 to 150 years ago, and for good reason. Turning back the clock will set up an encounter with the very complexities that led educators a century ago to search for better methods. Those who ignore history are, it is often said, doomed to repeat it.

The consequences of unfounded hysteria about declining school performance are more serious than spawning a few, misguided back-to-basics movements. Because popular indictment of school performance has been so devastating, many have concluded that the public education system itself is hopeless, leading to demands for privatization of education, whether with vouchers, contracting out to for-profit educators, or the quasi-privatization of charter schools. A few advocates of these alternatives may deliberately misstate the record on public school performance to advance their agenda. But most are genuinely confounded by the unreliability of data and information. Not surprisingly, alternatives to public education are widely judged on the basis of anecdotal evidence and exaggeration to be successful, though there are no data by which outcomes in public and private schools can be compared using adequate statistical controls for student characteristics.

If we Americans truly want to improve our schools, not destroy them, we must begin with a realistic appraisal of what they accomplish. The first step in any reform program is to figure out what the facts are. The following chapters attempt to put these facts in perspective.

1.

Our Failing Public Schools

Everyone seems to know that our schools are in desperate need of reform. The quality of public education seems to have declined, and schools are not up to the task of readying young people for the challenges of the next century. An apparently watered-down curriculum ensures that all students, regardless of whether they have mastered necessary skills, can graduate. "Social promotion" without requirements to master grade-appropriate skills is now commonplace, so even elite colleges must run "remedial" courses for freshmen in basic math and literacy, and business executives complain that high school graduates are ill-prepared for even relatively unskilled jobs.

Everyone seems to know that keeping teenagers from dropping out has become the primary purpose of high schools, which have shifted away from core academic instruction, attempting to keep young people interested with less rigorous alternatives. Instead of teaching basic skills, schools appear to concentrate on "self-esteem" and "values clarification," although they have discarded traditional values along with traditional skills, so that students no longer absorb the moral values that schools once inculcated.

Everyone seems to know as well that schools have abandoned traditional phonics reading methods that teach the alphabet so children can sound out words until they achieve fluency. Instead, teachers encourage children to commit "word pictures" to memory or, worse, let them pretend to read and even invent the meaning as they go along.

Professional educators evidently impose these unproven methods despite demands for phonics instruction by parents and many reading experts. Because better-educated parents are better prepared to teach their children to read, the abandonment of phonics may affect poor children most of all.

Math can be hard work for some children, so modern teaching attempts instead to entertain, ignoring drill in arithmetic, memorization of multiplication tables, and the mechanics of long division.

Everyone seems to know that immigrant children suffer most from schools' confusion of purpose since minority group advocates have pressured school systems, as well as Congress, to require bilingual education in order to maintain native languages and cultures. While public schools once "Americanized" students, conditioning them for an English-speaking job market, today's immigrant children reportedly complete public school unable to speak, read, or write English and unprepared to function in the national economy.

Former Xerox chairman and Bush administration assistant education secretary David Kearns concludes that "public education has put this country at a terrible competitive disadvantage. . . . If current . . . trends continue, American business will have to hire a million new workers a year who can't read, write or count."

"The vast majority of Americans," says Education Secretary Richard Riley, "do not know that they do not have the skills to earn a living in our increasingly technological society and international marketplace."

Louis Gerstner, chairman of IBM and host of a 1996 state governors' "summit" on education goals, says we need to improve our skills "if Americans are to succeed in the world marketplace," but since the education reforms begun by an earlier governors' conference in 1989, school performance has mostly "gotten worse." "Yeah," concludes Reagan administration education secretary William Bennett, "we're dumber than we thought we were."[1]

Most Americans agree with these indictments, although they are not sure what to do about them. Most adults remember that when they were students, public schools were safer, more academically serious, and focused both on basic learning and on more advanced thinking skills. They believe schools now do worse, even though a modern economy demands they do better. But this story, whatever partial truths it contains, is more a culturally embedded fable that has remained mostly unchanged for a century than a factual account.

Warnings like those of executives Gerstner and Kearns and education officials Bennett and Riley are now routine. But if schools are worse today than they used to be, then when, exactly, was the golden—or at least silver—age of education?

THE 1960S AND 1970S

Was it in the 1960s and 1970s? In 1974, best-selling author Vance Packard worried, "Are we becoming a nation of illiterates? [There is an] evident sag in both writing and reading . . . at a time when the complexity of our institutions calls for ever-higher literacy just to function effectively." He warned in *Reader's Digest* that "there is indisputable evidence that millions of presumably educated Americans can neither read nor write at satisfactory levels."[2]

Perhaps Packard was right and a decline in student achievement had begun a full generation earlier. But what were critics saying during that prior generation? A 1961 report by the Council for Basic Education claimed that a third of ninth graders could read at only a second or third grade level because phonics had been abandoned. Entitled *Tomorrow's Illiterates: The State of Reading Instruction Today*, the report included an essay by Dean Jacques Barzun of Columbia University, who noted that many of his graduate students "need coaching in the elements of literacy . . . , [partly because of] the loss of proper pedagogy in the lower schools."[3]

Attacks on the abandonment of phonics continued throughout the 1960s. Jeanne Chall's *Learning to Read: The Great Debate* was published in 1967,[4] then reissued in 1983. The press often reported surveys demonstrating deteriorating literacy. According to a 1960 Harris poll, only 10 percent of Americans considered themselves "avid book readers." A Gallup poll two years later reported that just 21 percent looked at books even casually.[5]

THE 1950S

Okay, so how about the 1950s? Today people look back on that decade as a time when schools did their job well, but contemporary observers were not impressed. Hannah Arendt warned in 1958 that academic standards "of the average American school lag . . . far behind the average standards in . . . Europe."[6]

Life magazine agreed. A multipart series on the "crisis" in American education[7] profiled two students: an American eleventh grader in one of our best middle-class public schools and a tenth grader in the Soviet Union. While Chicago's Stephen Lapekas was reading Robert Louis Stevenson's *Kidnapped*, Moscow's Alexei Kutzkov had studied English as a foreign language and completed works by Shakespeare and George Bernard Shaw. For the American, *Life* noted that "getting educated seldom seems too serious," but for the Russian, high grades were "literally more important than anything else in his life." Concluding that "U.S. high school students are . . . ignorant of things [elementary] school students would have known a generation ago," *Life* wondered how we could hope to win the cold war.[8]

In 1961, decades before William Bennett embarked on a similar crusade, Max Rafferty, a California district superintendent of schools preparing to enter politics as a Republican education reformer, declared in a *Reader's Digest* article that teachers "have been brainwashed for a quarter of a century with slogans like: 'There are no eternal verities'; 'Everything is relative'; 'Teach the child, not the subject'; and—worst of all—'Nothing is worth learning for its own sake.'"[9]

In 1958, historian Arthur Bestor complained in a *U.S. News and World Report* interview that physics, chemistry, and mathematics were now "taught to a shrinking proportion of students":

> Our standard for high school graduation has slipped badly. Fifty years ago a high-school diploma meant something. . . . We have simply misled our students and misled the nation by handing out high-school diplomas to those who we well know had none of the intellectual qualifications that a high-school diploma is supposed to represent—and does represent in other countries. It is this dilution of standards which has put us in our present serious plight.[10]

The launch of Sputnik in 1957 accelerated complaints about declining standards, but educational hand-wringing was even then nothing new. Bestor published his best-selling *Educational Wastelands: The Retreat from Learning in Our Public Schools* in 1953. A 1955 best-seller, Rudolf Flesch's *Why Johnny Can't Read* (reissued in 1986), warned that the refusal to use proven phonics methods "is gradually destroying democracy in this country; it returns to the upper middle class the privileges that public education was supposed to distribute evenly. . . ."[11]

In 1957, the *Saturday Evening Post* derided what it described as a typical, middle-class elementary school for setting up a school bank "to help teach what it calls 'the social phase' of arithmetic." The mathematics curriculum consisted of "electing young bank presidents, taking turns being cashiers, and standing in line at the cardboard play bank the children built."[12] (So much for memorizing multiplication tables!) A proficiency test given in 1951 to Los Angeles eighth graders found that more than half could not calculate an 8 percent sales tax on an $8 purchase. A *Time* magazine account was headed "Failure in Los Angeles." Local newspapers focused on another shocking disclosure: "330 of L.A. High Schools' Juniors Can't Tell Time."[13]

Surely, one might think, at least 1950s schools were safe. But a 1958 *Life* magazine cover story charged that students in American cities "terrorize teachers . . . [and] it often takes physical courage to teach."[14] A former teacher, Evan Hunter, fictionalized his experiences, including student assaults on teachers, in a 1953 book, *Blackboard Jungle*,[15] which was made into a film starring Glenn Ford and Sidney Poitier. Its screenplay was nominated for an Academy Award.

The 1940s

In the 1940s Americans were also convinced that academic achievement had plummeted. A survey of business executives conducted during the decade found that by large margins they believed recent graduates were inferior to the previous generation in arithmetic, written English, spelling, geography, and world affairs. In only one domain were recent graduates deemed superior: "poise."[16]

Atlantic Monthly published a suburban Sharon, Massachusetts, school board member's explanation of why even he had given up on public schools in the late 1940s: "If you find . . . your child cannot read or calculate half as well as you could at his age . . . you can do what other worried parents have done: mortgage your house [to put your child in a good private school]."[17]

Educators should return to the "three 'r's" rather than focusing on students' feelings and beliefs, urged the newsletter of the National

Council for American Education in 1950; "Emotional stability and attitudes and beliefs have always been considered—and we still believe them to be—the responsibilities of mothers and fathers," not schools. The superintendent of the Pasadena, California, schools was then fired after parents protested his de-emphasis of basic skills in favor of affective subject matter—a pedagogical practice remarkably similar to what upsets many Americans today who believe that such educational concepts are relatively new.

The Pasadena fight attracted national attention and typified battles throughout the country in which concerns about progressive pedagogy were mixed with McCarthyite paranoia about Communist influences in the teaching profession. In 1952 the journal *Progressive Education* summarized the most common complaints about schools: "attacks on textbooks that encourage inquisitive thinking and individual reasoning, . . . [m]ounting pressure to eliminate the 'frills and fads'—by which are meant such vital services as nurseries, classes for the handicapped, testing and guidance, programs to help youngsters understand and appreciate their neighbors of different backgrounds [then called 'brotherhood' education, not today's 'multiculturalism']. . . ."[18]

Warnings that school failures doomed the next generation to political or economic catastrophe were as common in the 1940s as today. *New York Times* education editor Benjamin Fine declared in his widely acclaimed 1947 book, *Our Children Are Cheated*, "Education faces a serious crisis. . . . We will suffer the consequences of our present neglect of education a generation hence."[19] Talking about airline reservation clerks he hired during World War II, a corporate training director complained that he had to "organize special classes to instruct them in . . . making change. . . . Only a small proportion [can] place Boston, New York, . . . Chicago, . . . Denver . . . in their proper sequence from east to west, or name the states in which they [are located]."[20]

Automatic advancement to the next grade before students mastered skills of their current one was the focus of a heated mid-1940s controversy over "social promotion." A 1944 article quipped that "passing pupils" was "passing the buck."[21]

Quizzing students about American history has always been a surefire way to prove declining standards. In 1987, Chester Finn, a Reagan administration education official, and Diane Ravitch, a Columbia University professor, published a best-selling book on the subject, *What Do Our 17-Year Olds Know?*[22] Very little, they concluded. But back in

1943, the *New York Times* developed a social studies test and administered it to seven thousand college freshmen nationwide. Only 29 percent knew that St. Louis was located on the Mississippi; only 6 percent knew the thirteen original states of the Union. Some thought Lincoln was the first president. The results, the *Times* reported, revealed a "striking ignorance of even the most elementary aspects of United States history."[23]

Walter Lippmann shared this concern when, in 1940, he addressed the American Association for the Advancement of Science: "During the past forty or fifty years those who are responsible for education have progressively removed from the curriculum . . . the western culture which produced the modern democratic state."[24]

World War I through the 1930s

During the Great Depression, abandonment of phonics was considered a major cause of schools' well-known deterioration. A 1938 study of first-grade teaching professed that contemporary elementary "teachers . . . conspire against pupils in their efforts to learn; these teachers appear to be determinedly on guard never to mention a letter by name, . . . or to show how to use either letter forms or sounds in reading."[25]

In the 1920s, business leaders reported dismay that educational preparation had become inadequate for the job market. The National Association of Manufacturers charged in 1927 that 40 percent of high school graduates could not perform simple arithmetic or accurately express themselves in English.[26] Woodrow Wilson appointed a presidential commission to study vocational education and international competitiveness in 1913. Its discovery that the United States (with fifteen times the population) had fewer vocational schools than Bavaria alone helped mobilize support for the Smith-Hughes Act of 1917, the first federal "voc-ed" legislation.[27]

More than half the young men recruited by the army during World War I "were not able to write a simple letter or read a newspaper with ease." An analyst at the time reported that the "overwhelming majority of these soldiers had entered school, attended the primary grades where reading is taught, and had been taught to read. Yet, when as adults they were examined, they were unable to read . . . simple material."[28]

The Early 1900s

In 1909, Ellwood P. Cubberly, the dean of Stanford's education school, wrote that, in an ever more interdependent world economy, "whether we like it or not, we are beginning to see that we are pitted against the world in a gigantic battle of brains and skill." His book, *Changing Conceptions of Education*, warned that Americans were coming up short in this contest.[29]

In 1902, the editors of the *New York Sun* opined that when *they* had attended school, children "had to do a little work. . . . Spelling, writing and arithmetic were not electives, and you had to learn." Now, however, schooling was "a vaudeville show. The child must be kept amused and learns what he pleases."[30] An *Atlantic Monthly* article of 1909 complained that basic skills instruction had been displaced in schools by "every fad and fancy" and noted that the curriculum resembled "the menu card of a metropolitan restaurant."[31] Although the phrasing was more quaint, the indictment was nearly identical to that of a 1985 book denouncing the curricular eclecticism of contemporary education—*The Shopping Mall High School*.[32]

The Nineteenth Century

Surely, one may think, there is an important respect in which proclamations of crisis are unique to the present: the transformation of American colleges into mass institutions must be responsible for complaints that universities are now forced to remediate secondary school failures. Yet Harvard's Board of Overseers, shocked at entering students' preparation, published samples of freshman writing to embarrass secondary schools in 1896. The Harvard professor who authored the board report wrote that there was "no conceivable justification for using the revenues of Harvard College" to instruct undergraduates who were unprepared for college work.[33] Another overseers' report, five years earlier, had found that only 4 percent of students who applied for Harvard admission could write an essay, spell, or properly punctuate a sentence.[34]

An 1898 writing exam at the University of California (Berkeley) found that 30 to 40 percent of entering freshmen were not proficient in English. Seemingly unaware that such a substantial proportion of admitted students flunked college readiness tests at the turn of the century,[35] the University of California's Policy Committee to Assist Unprepared Students reported in 1981 that "we are convinced, by test score trends, basic skills course enrollment trends, and anecdotal evidence, that a decline in the skill level of UC's entering freshmen has occurred."[36]

Bilingual education controversies also have nineteenth-century origins. Wisconsin's gubernatorial election turned on the issue of bilingual education in 1890. A massive mobilization of newly naturalized immigrant voters succeeded in ousting the Republican incumbent, William Hoard, who favored English for all children at a time when public schools in immigrant communities often taught only, or primarily, in German. The campaign led to the subsequent domination of Wisconsin politics by Democrats. Nonetheless, continuing nationwide complaints about bilingual education peaked a generation later, fed by anti-German prejudices stemming from World War I. Although a 1923 Supreme Court ruling prohibited states from requiring that all instruction, even in private schools, be in English,[37] the decision did little to stem the nativist tide.

One can go even further back to find complaints about scandalous school quality. America's first standardized test was administered in 1845 to a select group of Boston's brightest students (called "brag scholars" by the testing committee). Yet only 45 percent of these top fourteen-year-olds knew that water expands when it freezes. More disturbing, according to Massachusetts secretary of public instruction Horace Mann, Boston's schools were ignoring higher-order thinking skills; what little students knew came from memorizing "words of the textbook, . . . without having . . . to think about the meaning of what they have learned." Thus, 35 percent knew from history classes that, prior to the War of 1812, the United States had imposed an embargo on British and French shipping, but few had any clue what "embargo" meant. In one school, 75 percent of the students knew the date of the embargo, but only 5 percent could define the term.[38]

Lest the reader conclude that, if not well educated, at least young people once were better behaved, Mann also reported that three hundred Massachusetts teachers were forced by riotous and violent students to flee their classrooms in a single twelve-month period—the school year of 1837.[39]

Evidently, to cite a variation on a Will Rogers adage, "The schools ain't what they used to be and probably never were."[40]

2.

It Just Doesn't Add Up

If students learn less today than their parents did in the 1950s and 1960s, and if their parents learned less than their own parents learned in the 1930s and 1940s, and so forth, then at some point, going back far enough, one should discover an age when all students learned to read, calculate, and think, when citizenship was exercised from an appreciation of history and public values were formed through a study of great literature, when schools stuck to their mission of education and students knew how to behave. In fact, if the calendar is scrolled back far enough, one should even come to an age when employers and colleges did not complain about the quality of high school graduates, or when all high school grads knew how to make change.

But such an age never was. In 1900, for example, only 6 percent of all young people graduated from high school; more than half failed to get as far as eighth grade.[1] "Reading," as we know it today, was barely taught. What it meant then was standing in place and reading aloud; whether children understood what they recited was incidental.[2] Many World War I recruits failed a basic written intelligence test partly because, even if they had attended a few years of school and learned to read aloud, they were being asked by the Army to understand and interpret what they read, a skill many of them had never learned. The approved mode of instruction for many children, until "progressive education" began to have an impact in the 1920s, was "recitation"—repeating memorized historical or scientific facts, with the understanding of those facts considered less important.[3]

While the story of declining school quality across the twentieth century is, for the most part, a fable, equally unreliable have been predictions of economic, political, and military catastrophe likely to befall Americans, whose education purportedly lagged behind our competitors'. Despite a widespread belief in the inferiority of our schools in each era, America had the technological and managerial prowess to win not only the Second World War but the cold war as well. With an educational system allegedly trailing that of the Soviet Union, the Europeans, and lately the Japanese, the United States became the world's industrial, technological, and military leader and remains so in each of those realms today. When Walter Lippman, Hannah Arendt, Jacques Barzun, Vance Packard, and business leaders in every prior decade of this century predicted political and economic doom from our deficient (and deteriorating) school system, it turns out they were wrong.

An obsession with the quality of our schools accelerated in the 1980s, when most economic analysts believed the American economy was less healthy than either Western Europe's or Japan's. This country had high unemployment, frightening trade and fiscal deficits, and a low savings rate relative to those others. Most traumatic was the penetration of American automobile and office equipment markets by Japanese imports. In 1991, Americans told pollsters by nearly a three-to-one margin that they thought Japan was a stronger economic power than the United States. A workforce unprepared by public education to hold its ground was the most frequently named culprit. Best-selling books preached that inferior American schools doomed the American economy to lose a "head to head" race, as Lester Thurow put it, with our European and Asian "competitors."[4]

Now, in 1998, by the same three-to-one margin Americans tell pollsters they believe the United States to be stronger.[5] Few commentators decry U.S. "competitiveness" vis-à-vis Japan and Europe. Our fiscal deficit has disappeared and unemployment is now low. In 1997, economies of Asian nations like Korea (whose education system we had come to envy) "tanked" in mountains of bad debt, real estate speculation, and overcapacity. Nobody, however, thinks that these reversals of economic fortune were caused by a sudden reform of our educational system or by the sharp deterioration of schools in Japan, Germany, or Korea. The truth is, they were not. But it also must be true either that our school system has something to do with the fact that American workers have long been at least as productive, if not more so, than workers elsewhere, or that the role education plays in industrial power is exaggerated. In fact, both are the case.

That American opinion has been wrong about schools in the past does not, of course, mean that it is wrong today. This is a new and different era. William Bennett and Richard Riley, David Kearns and Louis Gerstner, Chester Finn and Diane Ravitch may have a better insight into the state of our schools and America's competitive situation than the doomsayers had in prior years—although one ought to be skeptical, because many of today's school critics are singing from the same hymnal they themselves used in the 1980s and early 1990s, when their warnings about an international "competitiveness" crisis proved to be unfounded. Nonetheless, the perceptiveness of today's school critics cannot be evaluated by their track record alone. It is possible that American education gradually improved until the mid-1960s, but since that time, as modern critics would have it, quality has declined. History offers us no formula for interpreting the present. But awareness of earlier blindness suggests caution about the bases used to draw contemporary conclusions. Knowing that a mistake has been made again and again in twentieth-century America should make us especially careful not to repeat it once more.

Certainly, even if critics have, without sufficient justification, fallen prey to an all-too-American belief that schools once were better than they are now, this does not mean that schools today are as good as they could be, as good as they should be, or as good as they have to be to prepare students for productive lives in the twenty-first century. It may be that schools are no worse, or even better, than they used to be but still not good enough. But certainly, the ability to assess public school performance through a clearsighted reading of history and fact is affected by whether the power of America's "deteriorating school myth" has predisposed us to examine evidence selectively, assuring a nagging dissatisfaction with public schools whatever the reality may be.

There are two ways of gauging whether schools have deteriorated. One is anecdotal evidence: our own experience with high school graduates and younger students, our memories of what schools were like when we were young, and the experiences of other observers, reported to us in conversation, in books, and in the media. The other way is the statistics with which social scientists attempt to confirm anecdotes: careful analysis of data, including test scores, that describe how school outcomes have changed over time.

In public policy, empirical evidence based on both anecdotes and statistics is needed to paint a complete picture. But anecdotes and statistics are each in their own ways flawed, so policymakers must judge carefully how much weight to give to the types of information acquired. The unreliability of anecdotes alone is obvious, but statistical evidence is also imperfect because, despite the modern obsession with facts and data, such tools are inadequate for analysis of something as complex as public education. In many cases the data required to make intelligent judgments are unavailable, especially those that invoke historical comparisons. This problem is discussed in greater detail in the next chapter. For now, consider this problem:

Suppose one wanted to know if University of California students who took the freshman writing exam in 1898 were better or worse prepared for college than entering freshmen are today. It might make sense first to look at the writing tests taken by students in 1898 and compare them to modern tests. But tests from 1898 have long since been discarded. Imagine, however, that they were available and could be matched to contemporary student tests. How would a grader compare the differences in style and content between the two eras? And if they could be compared, further challenges loom: it is possible that (although there are no demographic data available to confirm this hunch) in 1898, University of California freshmen were an elite group, coming from the upper crust of the state's then sharply pointed pyramidal social structure. Today's freshmen reflect not only California's social elite but its broad middle class and many lower-middle-class and impoverished families as well. To what should the 1898 freshmen writing samples be compared—only to the writing samples of today's children of bank executives, mine engineers, newspaper publishers, and successful ranchers, corresponding to the student population a century ago? Or should the 1898 writing samples be compared with the essays of all California freshmen today? Once this was done, would society know anything useful about the relative effectiveness of comprehensive high schools today and the selective schools of a century ago in teaching young people how to write? Would Americans have a better sense of whether entering freshmen are of poorer academic quality now than they were then?

Consider a more contemporary example. I attended a large, lower-middle-class high school in Queens, New York, and graduated in 1959. In the past 40 years, Bayside High School has changed, but probably less so than most urban schools. So I have wondered how the academic achievement of today's students compares with that of my peers. There are, however, no standardized tests, or records of tests, given to Bayside High School students both in 1959 and today. There is a New York State Regents exam, but not all students took it in either period, and, besides, there is no way of knowing whether today's tests are harder or easier than the tests taken back then.

Even if comparable test data were available, how could one control for student background characteristics? Bayside High School today has large numbers of Asian immigrant students. Should their performance be compared to that of the mostly Irish, Italian, and Jewish students in the school forty years ago? The effectiveness of the school itself would probably explain only a small part of any differences found.

If comparable test data are unavailable, perhaps other indicators could be substituted. Perhaps disciplinary records would indicate something. But supposing there were more suspensions and expulsions from Bayside High School forty years ago than there are today, this might not mean that the school then was a more unruly place. Standards for expulsions have changed radically. Today, students can be expelled only for weapons and drug violations (for these, there is increasingly "zero tolerance"); forty years ago they could be expelled for less serious offenses but with more administrative discretion allowed. Further complicating the comparison, forty years ago students at risk of expulsion for less serious offenses were more likely to drop out before the opportunity to expel arose. Perhaps the commitment to universal high school graduation is now excessive and schools should be less hesitant to expel students today, but such considerations will not help determine what the expulsion rate today would be if yesterday's standards were in place.

As an alternative to procuring school records on which a comparison could be based, it might have been useful to obtain exam papers or essays from a 1959 Bayside High School class and compare them to exams or essays written today. Might it be possible to find a teacher (perhaps retired) who had kept a collection of student writing? I would look for a teacher who had papers not only from the college preparatory honors classes I was fortunate to attend but also from the nonacademic-track classes that enrolled about half my classmates. I could then ask a teacher today to assign the same exam or essay questions to a similar collection of students and could request that a third, independent teacher grade all the exams, 1959 and today mixed together, to see if the older students had higher or lower average scores. But I was able to find no teacher who kept papers from any students thirty-five or forty years ago.* Had I been able to do so, the experiment would still have been imperfect. Neither the high school nor any government statistical agency has data on the social and economic characteristics of Bayside High School's student body then or now (school boundaries, for example, are not congruent with census tracts for which demographic data can be obtained), so it cannot be known if today's students are more or less advantaged than those of 1959. In sum, there is simply no way to determine, based on data, whether Bayside High School is doing a more or less effective job of educating young people.

So I searched for anecdotal evidence. I did find some teachers at Bayside High School who had been around for all or most of those years. Each assured me that students today are less academically prepared and more unruly than students were thirty-five or forty years earlier. I took these assurances seriously but with an awareness that anecdotal evidence is also unreliable. As adults (even teachers) age, their tolerance for youth tends to wither. Good students from a prior generation may now stand out in teacher memories, so that older teachers now compare them with average or even below-average students today. And, like everyone else's, teachers' anecdotal accounts may be influenced by the cultural assumptions they make about schools, the conviction people share that, regardless of the evidence, things are getting worse, not better.

Anecdotal evidence is unreliable because people select the experiences they assume are typical, based on subconscious assumptions. They notice the sales workers who cannot make change but do not remember those who do. They marvel at a youngster's computer skills but do not infer from this that schools must be doing a better job of teaching math, logic, and reasoning. Yet in a nation that turns out 2.5 million high school graduates a year (out of 45 million students, with nearly 3 million teachers in 15,000 school districts), even the best system would graduate a range of competencies. We have no ability to record our varied contacts with young people in a mental database, plot the distribution, discard the outliers, and draw valid conclusions about the state of American schools. Instead, anecdotes and experiences that confirm

* If any reader of this volume knows a teacher in any school who has retained such a long-ago sample of student work, I'd like to get in touch to see if such an experiment might be conducted. (My email address is <rothstei@oxy.edu>.)

a culturally acceptable story are incorporated into it, while others are forgotten or disconnected from the theme.

We also cannot control our interpretation of experience for relevant background factors and selection bias. Many readers of this book (along with most public school critics) will have attended, as youths, stable, middle-class public schools where, like me, they were tracked into curricula for the college bound. It is to these experiences that we carelessly compare the inferior academic performance of today's students. When we think only of today's comparable students—those in "good," suburban public schools and tracks—we may be forced to acknowledge that they may be even better educated than we were. Many of us are impressed with some aspects of our own children's educations in "good" public high schools. These young people certainly know more math and read better literature than we did in high school in the 1950s and 1960s. But most consider the advantaged student of the present day to be "exceptional," not reflecting what we believe to be the self-evident failure of today's public schools. Instead, we compare our own relatively homogeneous, even segregated, school experiences to contemporary school experiences of children whose counterparts in earlier generations either dropped out of school or were tracked into custodial, nonacademic programs.

Several books have been published (and widely read) in recent years describing in glowing terms the accomplishments of public schools and teachers, sometimes in the most challenging circumstances and with the most hard-to-educate students. One of the best is *Among Schoolchildren* by Tracy Kidder. The book follows Chris Zajac, a hardworking, Irish-American teacher in Holyoke, Massachusetts—a teacher so dedicated that she traveled to Puerto Rico during her summer vacation the better to understand her students' cultural background—for a full year. Another example is *Small Victories* by Samuel Freedman; this followed, also for a full year, Jessica Siegel, an English teacher in one of New York City's most difficult high schools—a teacher whose ceaseless work to raise the aspirations of her immigrant students led her to accompany them, almost force them, to visit colleges they otherwise would not have dreamed they could attend. Although Siegel quit the teaching profession after Freedman wrote his book, she is not unique: I have encountered many teachers like her in my own investigations of urban public schools. A third notable book is *Possible Lives* by Mike Rose, recounting the author's travels to rich, poor, and middle-income children's classrooms where teachers are dedicated and children learn in every region of the country. A fourth is Jay Matthews's *Class Struggle*, a book that, while complaining that more should follow the examples set forth, describes some remarkable low-income schools that prepare surprisingly large numbers of students to pass advanced placement tests. Readers of these books come away impressed with the teachers and schools depicted but tend nonetheless to regard these teachers and schools as aberrations, and the accounts do not affect the general feeling that schools are not academically serious and do a poorer job than they should.

On the other hand, books like Emily Sachar's *Shut Up and Let the Lady Teach*, the reminiscences of a reporter who spent a year as a teacher in an urban school where administrators, students, and fellow teachers all conspired against education, or Charles Sykes' *Dumbing Down Our Kids*, a collection of stories from around the country about how "political correctness" and lack of standards have destroyed American schools, become popular evidence reinforcing preexisting convictions that schools are in crisis. More than sufficient anecdotes can be found to fill dozens of books to confirm or to refute the myth of public school failure. Which of these anecdotes one chooses to believe depends largely, if not entirely, on one's preconceptions.

Anecdotes about education can be useful to guide researchers' search for data, or to illustrate the data found. But anecdotes are no substitute for data. In 1988, *Stand and Deliver* was a successful, popular movie depicting the real-life struggles of Jaime Escalante, a teacher of Mexican-American students in Los Angeles, to inspire them to study for a calculus advanced placement exam. Most viewers concluded from the film that Escalante and his students were unique, not typical of other inner-city teachers and students (whom they knew from hearsay or from journalistic accounts to be educational failures). Yet, last year, more than five thousand College Board advanced placement tests were given to Hispanic students in Los Angeles; about half the scores were high enough for college credit. Is this number too few for a district with the size of Los Angeles's Hispanic and low-income population? Or is it more than should be expected from a school district with the enormity of Los Angeles's demographic and other challenges? These are much more difficult questions than the public debate about education usually entertains, and they cannot be answered with anecdotal books or feature films alone.

Perhaps the most common anecdotes are those told by employers who claim that high school graduates hired for entry-level jobs cannot read or write, or that when firms give employment tests requiring only a primary grade competency in reading or math, large numbers of applicants fail. When such stories are repeated so often, it is difficult to remain skeptical about their implications, especially when they are confirmed in our own experience by salespeople who are unable to make change. But skepticism is still necessary. As with the stories about great teachers and successful minority students, employer anecdotes about school successes contradict popular preconceptions, and so never penetrate public consciousness.

Consider two newspaper reports, published within a month of each other in late 1997. In one, Eastman Chemical chairman Earnest Deavenport bemoaned the skills of American workers and called for a "restructuring" of the public school system: "The shortage of skilled workers . . . could threaten the amazing growth and productivity gains of the past decade," he said.[6] Yet, in another report, Daimler-Benz chairman Juergen Schrempp said his company was undergoing a cultural "revolution" because of the teamwork ability and creativity of employees at Mercedes's new plant in Tuscaloosa, Alabama. Alabama employees not only showed the company that it was possible to delegate decisionmaking lower in the chain of command than was believed possible, but these employees are also now being sent to Germany to teach headquarters how to do it.[7] Each of these newspaper reports, one can assume, accurately reported the interpretations of Eastman or Daimler leaders regarding American workforce skills. But because of readers' preconceptions, they will more likely remember the views of Eastman's Mr. Deavenport than of Daimler's Mr. Schrempp.

Nor was the Daimler view unique. The American Vocational Association reports a speech by the apprenticeship director of Siemens, a German-based electronics firm that is the second-largest employer in the world. The Siemens manager noted that American youths (at plants in Florida, North Carolina, and Kentucky) scored higher on his company's apprenticeship exams than comparable German young people who followed the same curriculum and took the same tests.[8] His account generated no newspaper headlines about successful American schools. It inspired no commentators to proclaim that our schools were superior to Germany's. Yet Americans can hardly help but be aware, to take one example, of telephone company executives' claims that American high school graduates cannot pass basic employment tests. In a nation as large as ours, sufficient anecdotes can be recounted to prove any contention. That anecdotes supporting preconceptions are more likely to be publicized is not any kind of systematic evidence that such stories better reflect reality.

These employment-test anecdotes are suspect, among other reasons, because they are not based on representative or properly controlled samples. It is not known, for example, from the Siemens manager's speech whether Siemens's pay scales in the United States are relatively high while in Germany they are relatively low: if this were the case, it might be that Siemens's apprenticeship programs in America enticed the cream of our non-college-bound high school graduates, while similar programs in Germany attracted the less able. Likewise, when telephone company executives bemoan the low scores of test takers wanting operator jobs, their complaints rarely disclose what wage rates those jobs offered. If the wage was low enough, surely it appealed only to those job seekers who did poorly in school.

This much is known: average hourly wages of high school graduates declined dramatically in the past generation, from $12.17 in 1973 to $10.46 in 1995 (the dollars are adjusted for inflation).[9] During most of this period, unemployment was substantial and there was a surplus of high school graduates seeking jobs. These data may suggest some serious, noneducational problems with our economy, but because entry-level wages have correspondingly declined, it is apparent that employers of high school graduates have not felt it necessary to raise wages to attract a better-qualified workforce, despite their publicized complaints about skills deficits. When an actual survey of employers was conducted in 1990 by a commission headed by two former labor secretaries, Republican Bill Brock and Democrat Ray Marshall, it reported "we did not expect what we found . . . Education levels rarely seemed a concern." Despite the very vocal, headline-grabbing complaints of a few corporate executives, Brock and Marshall's commission concluded, there is an "evident absence of a serious shortage of people with strong cognitive skills."[10] (Employers did complain, on the other hand, of job applicants with poor work habits.)

The unreliability of anecdotal evidence is also confirmed by public opinion surveys. Polls consistently show that, while the public believes schools do a terrible job, respondents generally think the particular schools their own children attend are pretty good. Each year since 1969, Gallup has asked Americans to "grade" their public schools.

In the most recent survey, only 23 percent of parents of public school children gave the nation's schools a grade of A or B, 46 percent gave a grade of C, and 20 percent gave grades of D or F (11 percent said they had no opinion).[11] But when the same public school parents were asked to grade the schools their own children attended, they had a different view: nearly three times as many, 64 percent, gave grades of A or B, another 23 percent gave a grade of C, and only 11 percent gave a grade of D or F (2 percent declined to give an opinion).[12] These discordant results are not characteristic only of public school parents. When adults with no children in school were asked to rate the schools in their own neighborhoods, 42 percent gave a grade of A or B, but only 23 percent thought schools nationally deserved such grades.[13]

Gallup's pollsters have also asked respondents why they thought their own neighborhood schools were better than the nation's schools generally. Two-thirds believed that their own neighborhood schools place more emphasis on high academic achievement, have stronger discipline and less violence, enjoy more harmonious race relations, provide better special education programs for students with disabilities, send more students to college, suffer fewer dropouts, have finer athletic and extracurricular programs, and offer richer programs for gifted and talented students than do schools in the nation as a whole. In only one respect did respondents believe that their own neighborhood schools were inferior to others: of those who had an opinion, a majority claimed that, despite the superior results and programs of their local schools, these have less money to spend than do schools nationwide![14]

Similar results have been reported consistently since 1969. This dissonance is not unique to education: public opinion polls also find that voters hold Congress in very low esteem but are satisfied with their own representatives. In cases like these, where the public's view of an institution as a whole is more negative than its own experience with it, it is reasonably certain that popular opinion has been influenced by ideology, by broad cultural assumptions, and perhaps by the media's interpretations, not by a careful examination of evidence. The interpretations become self-fulfilling: newspapers, magazines, television, and business, political and academic leaders all insist that the schools are deteriorating. Swayed by this commentary, the public concludes likewise. The same experts then report growing dissatisfaction with public schools as evidence for their own claims.

In 1978, a CBS News survey found that 51 percent of blacks felt that schools had improved since they were children. Shortly afterward, a wave of condemnation of school performance began to accelerate, with public anguish focused on the schools black children attend—probably because the job and income prospects of blacks continued to lag so far behind those of whites. In 1983, only five years after the original CBS News survey, a *New York Times* poll found a markedly different impression—only 34 percent of blacks felt that schools had improved from the prior generation.[15]

Surely, in this brief interval the quality of schools blacks attended had not suddenly deteriorated to the point where it was worse than a generation before. What had changed was the ideological prism through which our experience is filtered. Worry grew about the nation's trade deficit with Japan, and journalists increasingly quoted business executives who put the blame on the alleged educational deficiencies of American workers. The Reagan administration commissioned a report, *A Nation at Risk*, that alleged a "rising tide of mediocrity" in American public education. So-called informed opinion had come to believe more strongly that schools had deteriorated, and black Americans, like everyone else, reinterpreted their memories to conform to policymakers' widely publicized views.

This shift in attitude by black survey respondents is especially telling: while it may be difficult to gather valid statistical evidence to measure changes in educational quality for the nation as a whole, there can be little doubt that the schools black children attended were dramatically better in 1980 than those attended by their parents in the 1950s and earlier, a period when much of the nation operated a dual (separate but hardly equal) school system. In 1950, for example, fewer than 13 percent of black males over the age of twenty-five had completed high school; only 25 percent had even completed the eighth grade. By 1980, 55 percent of adult black males were high school graduates.[16] So in this case, the belief of most black Americans that schools their children attended were worse than their own was a case of memory playing tricks. When told in 1983 that two-thirds of black adults now thought that schools were worse than they used to be, Vernon Jordan exclaimed: "Objectively, that's wrong. The child in the worst ghetto is getting a better education than I got in Daisy Allen High School in Atlanta. We only had one Bunsen burner and that only worked on Thursdays."[17]

Jordan's protest that the widely accepted fable of school deterioration is off-base does not mean that schools are good enough today, either for blacks or for other Americans. Though Cassandras of past years have proved mistaken, our nation may be facing a new economic or political challenge that cannot be overcome without school improvement. And even if there is no crisis, in a vital society most institutions should engage in ongoing self-examination and reform. The auto industry should always try to make a better car; computer manufacturers should improve their operating systems; hospitals should implement better procedures for patient care. It is not necessary to believe that cars are now falling apart, that computer quality is declining, or that people are getting sicker in order to support a quest for further improvement in these products and services.

Schools should be no exception: educators should explore better ways of organizing schools, delivering instruction, measuring results. But school reform is unique in one respect: our political culture cannot seem to proceed to reform education without believing that the present system is failing, that our schools are in crisis, that students are, on the whole, more poorly educated today than in the past. These beliefs are not necessary for reform to be effective. Like auto executives, software engineers, or health care administrators, policymakers could improve education without adopting the notion of a lost golden age. Reform could even be pursued with a conviction that schools now are better than they have ever been. But the nature of the century-long debate about school quality raises questions about whether school reform from a position of self-confidence may be beyond our national capacity.

It matters. If Americans believe their schools perform more poorly than they used to, reforms will be designed differently from reforms aimed to improve a satisfactory institution. It is difficult to make a careful assessment of schools' ills and successes, or to develop a plan to improve them, if myth gets in the way. The myth has led and will continue to lead to trying to fix the wrong things—to focusing on nonexistent problems while perhaps ignoring the real ones. Under popular pressure, the education community may mistakenly enact more radical reforms than it should, may seek "systemic" changes rather than incremental improvements, or may become so impatient for results that earlier reform programs are replaced with new ones, before prior measures have had a chance to take root. Our society may demoralize good teachers and schools by neglecting to appreciate their contributions, even while it sends a message to poor teachers and schools that inadequate performance is inevitable and should be tolerated. In fact, each of these unintended consequences has flowed from our hyperventilated denunciation of school failure.

It is important to learn, if possible, how school performance today compares with that of the past, and to strive to go beyond anecdotes in order to do so. Unfortunately, however, almost nothing that is statistically reliable can be gathered about the history of student achievement. Widespread claims of long-term school deterioration, as well as less widespread claims of long-term school improvement, have very little basis in verifiable fact.

3.

Evidence: Then and Now

If anecdotes and experience are unreliable guides to changes in student achievement, how can one know whether schools are "better" or "worse" than they once were? The best way would be to have a test, or group of tests, given to students in the past that could be administered to their counterparts today, so achievement "then" and "now" could be compared.

Unfortunately, however, problems like those encountered in the previous chapter very quickly grow when speculating on what evidence might be obtained to compare the quality of University of California freshmen in 1898 to that of modern-day freshmen, or what evidence might be used to measure Bayside High School achievement in 1959 against achievement today. Objective indicators simply do not exist.

There are very few test series that extend consistently back in time, though test scores have long been used to evaluate (and mostly condemn) American schools. In Chapter 1, it was noted that Horace Mann's committee of examiners administered the nation's first standardized test in 1845 to five hundred Boston fourteen-year-olds. The committee reported it "difficult to believe that there should be so many children . . . unable to answer, . . . so many absurd answers, so many errors in spelling, in grammar, and in punctuation." And when children did answer a question correctly, they frequently did not understand the answer they had given because, as the examining committee put it, the children had been taught "the name of the thing rather than the nature of the thing"; thus, the finding that Boston eighth grade students could name the date of Jefferson's embargo but not explain what "embargo" meant.

Unless today's eighth graders were asked the same questions Mann asked his, it is not possible to compare how well students learn today with how well they learned then. But, mostly, it would not be desirable to ask the same questions, even if feasible. (Questions from Mann's standardized science test: "How high can you raise water in a common pump, with a single box?"; "What is the altitude of a heavenly body?"[1]) Since Mann's time, American educators have always sought to improve their tests, by asking better questions and improving test conditions. And they have attempted to improve the nature of instruction by emphasizing different skills on the tests by which teaching is assessed.

Commercial testing firms (like Riverside Publishing, Macmillan, Houghton Mifflin, McGraw-Hill, Harcourt Brace) now compete to persuade education agencies to adopt their assessment systems. It is generally impossible to compare one of these tests to another—the only way to do so would be to conduct an expensive experiment whereby several tests were given to the same students and the scores compared. Even this would be misleading because different tests may, and usually do, emphasize different parts of the same curriculum, so some students may do better than others on one test and worse on another. Today's testing controversies concern, among other issues, the extent to which math tests should assess computational skills or understanding of theory or mathematical reasoning ability. Each available standardized test resolves this question somewhat differently, so students who score well on one are not necessarily comparable to students who score well on another.

The lack of comparability between tests means that when educators improve or change their tests, they may get a better handle on how well their schools are doing compared to other schools using the same test at the same time, but they lose the ability to compare their students with those of the past.

Even if identical tests were given to students at different times, misleading comparisons would still follow. Curricula change. If tests are to reveal something about school quality, they must be based on the topics being taught, not on outdated material of prior years. Even the most determined advocate of arithmetic drill (and opponent of "new math") must acknowledge that there are some mathematical concepts that must be taught today but were not in the past: set theory, for example. No test from the past, when set theory was not taught, if readministered today could help us compare achievement of today's students with those of yesterday. Further, to the extent schools spend any time teaching set theory (whether it is given too much or too little emphasis in schools today is not the point), they must necessarily spend less time drilling multiplication tables (or some other aspect of the prior curriculum). One should thus expect students to do somewhat less well on tests that assess arithmetic calculation skills alone.

Similarly, it is reasonable to expect today's high school students to know facts about the 1991 Gulf War, on which students twenty years ago could obviously not have been tested. By the same token, students today are likely to be somewhat less familiar with the events surrounding President Nixon's resignation than students were in 1975. Horace Mann tested Boston's students on "what was the result of the invasion of Canada by the Americans in the last war?" To recognize that today's students ought to be less familiar than Mann's students with 1812 military battles does not disparage the importance of "cultural literacy"; even the most determined advocate of a classical core curriculum will admit that, as history unfolds and our literary tradition evolves, the curriculum must adapt. Such admission forfeits the possibility of satisfactory correspondence between standardized tests administered in different periods.

Some skills are easier to test than others, and so tests may give an unrealistic picture of what students know compared to those in the past. For example, it is more difficult to test creative writing than to test spelling (as well as incomparably more expensive because it takes much longer to grade a writing exam and there is additional time and expense to ensure that assessments of different graders are consistent). If the curricular emphasis is placed on creative writing, drill in spelling may suffer. Or, what is worse, if the public demands higher test scores from schools, teachers may intensify their focus on the more easily tested spelling, at the expense of more difficult-to-test writing. Students tested after their classes stressed creative writing show a decline in literacy skills from previous student cohorts, when in fact their overall literacy may be superior. Many observers have noted that some recent test reports show greater declines in scores for upper grade students than for lower grade ones. Could this be because easier-to-test "basic skills" are more central to a lower-level curriculum, while advanced grades now concentrate more on difficult-to-test "higher order" skills than they once did? Or is this explanation simply an excuse for poor performance? No one knows.

We Americans are used to making snap judgments about our schools from test score reports but have little ability to judge the extent to which these scores reflect assumptions about the relative importance of different curricular emphases and skills. The Educational Testing Service (ETS) plays a role in this confusion. On the one hand, ETS (or its clients, like the Department of Education or the College Board) release test scores from the National Assessment of Educational Progress or SAT in simplistic summaries that contribute to misunderstanding. On the other, the ETS's own technical research frequently cautions against the conclusions inevitably drawn from such simplistic reports.

In one report worth citing in detail, ETS researcher Robert Mislevy explained how difficult test interpretation can be, utilizing the following example from the Olympics:[2] the decathlon is a medley of ten track and field events, like the hundred-meter dash, the long jump, and the shot put. It is simple to determine which athlete excels in a single event, for instance, who throws the javelin the farthest. But determining which athlete should win the decathlon requires a decision by experts about how each of the individual events should be weighted in the total. (Is two seconds faster in a sprinting event worth five feet farther in the shot put or four feet? Is a victory in the discus throw worth more or less than a victory in the long jump?) In 1932, the American athlete James Bausch won the decathlon because he won some events (the discus, shot put, javelin, and pole vault) by large margins, even though he did less well in running events. But in 1985 the Olympic Committee's experts changed the scoring of the decathlon so that an athlete who did exceptionally well in some events could not offset, in his total score, a relatively poorer showing in others. The new scoring table gave greater emphasis to well-roundedness, so that athletes who did relatively well in all events now got the higher scores. If the 1932 Olympic decathlon had been scored using 1985 standards, then the gold medal would not have gone to Bausch but rather to a Finn, Akilles Jarvinen. In comparing the scores of today's athletes to those from earlier in the century, should yesterday's scoring weights be used or today's? What if athletic training programs had changed to give greater emphasis to well-roundedness, but the technical rating systems had not kept up and scores continued to emphasize exceptional excellence in a few events? In this case, modern athletes who are deemed superior (by today's standards) would score lower than prior generations of athletes whose mix of skills is no longer valued. In academic testing, rarely is this kind of information about the relative importances of different skills or about how test questions match shifting curricular emphases obtainable, yet people are quick to form conclusions about changes in performance.

Even where there was a consistent test series over a reasonable time period, the tests were not likely to have been administered with an eye toward future intergenerational comparisons, and background data necessary for making such comparisons were not collected. Consider the much-criticized practice of "social promotion," where students are advanced a grade in school even if they have not fully mastered the previous grade's curriculum. Whether this is wise policy, it is clear that if schools promote students today more easily, students in any grade level will be younger on average than used to be the case. Should test scores of fourth graders today, when all are about nine years old and have had four years of schooling, be compared to test scores in the past when some fourth graders—the slowest learners—were ten, eleven, or twelve and might already have had five to seven years of school? If not, and if it is desirable to compare scores only of students who are the same age and who have been in school the same number of years, birth date information must be provided for each student whose test score is included. Few test series have collected such data, much less kept or analyzed them.

Other, more obvious background information is also unavailable. To make an accurate assessment of schools' comparative performance, it is important that the children being compared come from the same economic and social classes. In the mid-1960s, the federal government sponsored a massive school data collection project, headed by sociologist James S. Coleman. His report, *Equality of Educational Opportunity*, was revolutionary in its findings, and since its publication in 1966, education researchers have understood that a child's family and community characteristics have much to do with even a good school's ability to educate. The test scores of a school's students may have less to do with the school's academic effectiveness than with the social and economic characteristics children bring to that school.

Awareness has subsequently grown of how important these background characteristics are in determining student achievement.

Measured student achievement is the product of many socializing institutions, not just school alone. The most important of these is the family, whose influence is powerfully affected by parents' social and economic status as well as ethnic subcultural values and practices. Recent research has found, for example, that the language an infant hears in the first three months of life plays an important role in the child's later intellectual development. According to one study of children between the ages of thirteen months and three years, parents with professional occupations addressed an average of 2,153 words an hour to their children during those two years; working class parents directed an average of 1,251 words an hour to their children; and parents on welfare spoke an average of only 616 words an hour to their children.[3] Even a "head start" program for preschoolers would come too late to overcome entirely these initial differences. Much less can be learned than it appears by using test scores to compare the quality of a school whose students come from professional families to one whose students are working class.

Prenatal and infant nutrition also play a role. So does family structure—some research has shown that in families with fewer siblings, children experience more intellectual stimulation at home (because their environment has a higher proportion of adults) than do children in larger families. Children whose parents attended school longer (regardless of the quality of those schools) tend to have better test results, perhaps because those parents, no matter what they learned, came to value the importance of education. If this is the case, dropout prevention programs may have their biggest impact in the subsequent generation.

There is general recognition that cultural values play a role in achievement. It is not an accident that the offspring of some (but not all) Asian ethnic groups tend to excel more than many others in school; although these patterns are evident, no one can fully explain them. Researchers believe that single parenthood has a negative impact on children's achievement, and that children born to very young mothers can be expected to perform less well academically than children born to adult mothers.

Economic considerations are important. One cause of poor academic performance by inner-city children is their unstable housing conditions; because they move frequently, changing schools and teachers, they cannot benefit from consistent instruction. Children in communities where good job opportunities are limited, even for those who stay in school, may conclude that school success is not worthwhile, and this will certainly have an impact on their motivation and their achievement. One of the Coleman Report's findings was that an important influence on student achievement was a child's "sense of control of the environment" because an unconscious faith that the world is not capricious, and that effort is fairly rewarded, is both necessary for school success and more likely to be found in children whose families are economically comfortable and who have not experienced a history of discrimination. Finally, Coleman and subsequent researchers have concluded that a critical determinant of student achievement is "contextual"—the average family characteristics (taking all the measures just named) of the other children with whom a student goes to school. A child, no matter how disadvantaged, who attends a school mainly populated by privileged children may, other things being equal, do better in school than an advantaged student who attends a school populated mainly by children who are less well endowed with what Coleman called "social capital."

Increased sophistication about the multiple nonschool influences on student achievement does not imply an iron determinism. The fact that even the best school will in most cases find it easier to improve the achievement of children whose parents are college graduates than to do likewise for those whose parents are high school dropouts is not negated by findings that some bright children of high school dropouts who attend the worst schools will do better on achievement tests than typical children of college graduates who attend the best schools. Our understanding of the interaction between school practices and family characteristics is still too primitive to permit a full understanding of why and under what circumstances these various outcomes occur. Consider the finding that infants in professional families hear, on average, more spoken words than infants in working-class families. While this may help explain social class differences in academic achievement, it was also found that some working-class infants heard more spoken words than some infants in professional households, while some infants in welfare households heard more spoken words than those in working-class homes. It simply is not known if the poor children who progress beyond their peers come from families that are unusually verbal for their social class, if they experienced especially effective schools or teachers, or if they simply had more motivation or native ability.

Knowledge of the important relationships of family, community, and contextual characteristics to student achievement does not make better schools impossible, but it does mean that school improvement efforts must take these linkages into account in designing practical reform programs and realistic goals. Clearly, no matter what goals society posits for typical children and how successful it is in achieving them, there will always be a distribution of outcomes—if the goals are not trivial, some students will perform below them, while others will perform above them.

A most intelligent assessment of these problems came from, of all people, Terrel Bell, secretary of education in the Reagan administration, whose 1983 report *A Nation at Risk* did so much to ignite hysteria about schools in the 1980s and who reinforced this sense of alarm with annual press conferences to publicize "wall charts" calling attention to purportedly declining test scores. Reflecting ten years later on the damage these initiatives had wrought, Bell said,

> We had placed too much confidence in school reforms that affected only six hours [a day] of a child's life. . . . In the face of many negative influences on our children that come from outside the school, we have done well to maintain our high school completion rate and our level of performance on achievement measures. . . . We have foolishly concluded that any problems with the levels of academic achievement have been caused by faulty schools staffed by inept teachers.[4]

Acceptance of the fact that schools are only one influence on student achievement should not be taken to suggest that this influence is unimportant. School improvement can still have impact. But sophistication about the social conditions that help shape performance in school does render historical comparisons of student achievement almost useless unless there are adequate data to compare the achievement of students whose family, community, and contextual characteristics have been similar in different periods.

Before the Coleman Report demonstrated that school performance cannot be measured in isolation, school administrators and researchers frequently contended with persistent claims of declining student performance by conducting "then and now" studies of education. In reading through the educational research literature of the past, one cannot help but be struck by the consistently defensive tone of these studies: professors or school district administrators began their published reports by recounting the denunciations of schools by politicians, journalists, academics, pundits, or parent groups who had claimed that "today's" schools did not measure up to the standards of the past, that teachers no longer instructed children in basic skills, and that young people knew less than they once did. The professors or administrators exclaimed that they had been subjected to this abuse long enough, and therefore they had combed school district archives for tests given to students several decades earlier. The researchers then described administering these outdated tests to students, under conditions as similar to the past as possible. The reports almost always concluded by showing the contemporary scores to be superior, refuting the conventional wisdom of the day.

While most (though not all) of these "then and now" studies were methodologically unsophisticated, and while careful social scientists today would never sanction such uncontrolled (for background characteristics) research, the history of these studies sheds a useful light on the unchanging debates about the quality of American education. Further, assuming, not unreasonably, that demographic and other social changes may not have been as rapid during the periods covered by these earlier studies as today, the studies suggested that school critics of the past were mistaken.

There have been several dozen such investigations; only a few typical ones will be described here. In 1925, Otis Caldwell, a school director and Columbia Teachers College professor in New York, and Stuart Courtis, director of teacher training at Detroit Teachers College, noted that "survey after survey has revealed unsuspected inadequacy or inefficiency in American education," resulting in "superintendents and teachers [being] dismissed" and "school systems and methods [being] reorganized." Caldwell and Courtis determined to "bring a long-delayed message of encouragement to all who have participated in accomplishing the educational progress of the last fifty years." To do so, they readministered Horace Mann's 1845 Boston test to a national sample ("from Maine to California") of eighth graders in 1919.[5]

Mann's test questions that had retained curricular relevance seventy-five years later were selected. (Questions like those asking for the height of a heavenly body, or about the invasion of Canada in the "last war," were dropped.) Caldwell and Courtis printed a new exam with the remaining questions and invited school districts to participate. School superintendents from forty-six states volunteered. Unlike the Mann test, which had been given only to "brag scholars" (students whom Mann described as "the flower of the Boston schools"), the superintendents agreed to test all eighth graders who were present on the day the exam was given. Twelve thousand entries were returned for scoring.[6]

Caldwell and Courtis found that, despite administering the test to the full range of eighth graders, not only the brightest as in 1845, the contemporary students had more success. Their median score on the relevant questions was 45.5 percent, against 37.5 percent for pupils back in 1845. The investigators concluded that children of their own day did somewhat worse than the earlier children on "pure memory" questions and somewhat better on the "thought or meaningful questions." To illustrate with an example used earlier in this report, the researchers reported that "in 1845, 35% of the children knew the year when the embargo was laid by President Jefferson, but only 28% knew what an embargo was. In 1919, only 23% knew the year, but 34% knew the meaning."[7]

In 1934, a Los Angeles school researcher, Elizabeth Woods, gave a sixth grade reading test to students in 33 elementary schools where the same test had been administered ten years earlier. She found that scores were half a grade higher in 1934 than they had been in 1924.[8]

In 1946, Don Rogers, a Chicago assistant school superintendent, tired of hearing "employers . . . allege that present-day pupils (even high school graduates) are not proficient. . . . The imputation is that . . . our school system formerly trained them better than now."[9] So Rogers readministered a sixth grade arithmetic test from 1923. He found that the 1946 pupils on average scored about the same as 1923 pupils (despite the unusually high teacher turnover the 1946 students had experienced during World War II, as well as the constant disruptions caused by wastepaper, soap, and other wartime drives conducted in schools) and declared that the exercise "discounts the allegations that . . . Chicago pupils of an earlier generation did better work than their sons and daughters who are now in the elementary schools."

In 1948, Springfield, Missouri, schools came under attack from a citizens group for embracing tenets of "progressive education" and for ignoring the teaching of basic skills, particularly in reading. University of Illinois professors F. H. Finch and V. W. Gillenwater undertook a study to "reveal whether the teaching of reading had increased or decreased in effectiveness," by giving a 1931 sixth grade reading test to contemporary sixth graders in the same Springfield schools. They found that 1948 students had higher scores, concluding that "apparently reading instruction . . . is now more effective . . . and most sixth grade children now in schools do better in reading than did their predecessors."[10] While Finch and Gillenwater did not use formal statistical controls that would be expected in similar research today, they superficially investigated the characteristics of 1931 and 1948 students and determined that the occupational classifications of the parents were similar in the time periods studied.

Tests of General Educational Development (GED) are used as an alternative high school certification for students who drop out. They were originally developed by the army in 1943 to assess the academic skills of draftees. To establish a scoring scale, the army arranged for the test to be administered to a representative sample of 35,000 seniors in 814 high schools across the country (representative except that, in states with segregation, only white schools were included). In 1955, at a time of ferocious popular criticism of the public schools (the belief that schools had deteriorated was as widespread as it is today), army officials wondered if the 1943 scale was still appropriate. So the Department of Defense contracted with the University of Chicago to conduct a new study, giving a 1955 GED test to a similarly representative national group of high school seniors. Then a smaller sample of students was given both the 1943 and 1955 tests, so that the scales on the two could be "equated." The Chicago professor who analyzed the results, Benjamin Bloom, reported that "in each of the GED tests the performance of the 1955 sample of Seniors is higher than the performance of the 1943 sample. . . . In mathematics the average senior tested in 1955 exceeds 58 percent of the students tested in 1943." (Average performance also exceeded earlier scores in natural sciences, reading, English, and social studies.) "These differences are not attributable to chance variation in test results," Bloom concluded, but "indicate that the high schools are doing a significantly better job of education in 1955 than they were doing in 1943."[11]

In the early 1950s, Vera Miller and Wendell Lanton, researchers working for the Evanston, Illinois, school district, noted that parents and educators often charged that "too much time [is] being devoted to music, arts, crafts, dramatics and unit work [group projects] to the detriment of the 'Three R's.'" In response, Miller and Lanton reprinted the standardized reading tests that had been given twenty years earlier in the district and used them to examine contemporary students. Like Finch and Gillenwater in Missouri several years earlier, they had no formal statistical controls for background characteristics, but they observed that the "community was relatively stable [and] present day groups of pupils and those of the past were similar in most respects. . . . The area contains a cross section of people of different races and of varied social and economic status." To ensure the most practically consistent test conditions, the district's testing director from the 1930s also administered the test in the 1950s, using similar procedures. The 1950s tests were given on or near the same day of the month as the 1930s tests. Miller and Lanton tested third, fourth, and eighth graders from 1952 to 1954 and found that, for example, fourth graders in 1952 scored six months ahead in reading comprehension and were eight months more advanced in vocabulary than their 1932 counterparts. "Present day pupils read with more comprehension and understand the meaning of words better than did children who were enrolled in the same grades and schools more than two decades ago," Miller and Lanton deduced.[12]

In 1976, the Indiana state superintendent of public instruction, Harold Negley, teamed up with two Indiana University professors, Roger Farr and Leo Fay, to examine the state's reading instruction. Their report notes that "the charge is sometimes made that children do not read as well as in the past and that schools are to blame."[13] In 1945, the state had administered a standardized reading test to a sample of 25 percent of its students at each grade level. So in 1976, Farr, Fay, and Negley reprinted the 1945 tests for the sixth and tenth grades, and gave them to a comparable sample of students. The new sample, though representing only 7 percent of the state's students in those grades, was selected to take account of the state's regional diversity and urban-rural-suburban distribution, so that the makeup of test takers in the two time periods was as similar as possible. Their raw results revealed that sixth and tenth graders in 1976 read at virtually the same level as their counterparts in 1945. The average 1945 sixth grader read at exactly the national sixth grade norm that had been established in 1943, while the average 1976 sixth grader read at one-tenth of one month below the 1943 sixth grade norm.

The state of Indiana, however, had kept unusually good records on the students who took the 1945 test, and Farr, Fay, and Negley noted that these students were considerably older than the sixth and tenth grade students who took the test in 1976. In the earlier era, it was more common not to promote students who achieved below grade level; in 1976, the sixth grade included eleven- and twelve-year-olds almost exclusively, but in 1945 there had been many thirteen- and fourteen-year-olds in the sixth grade as well. In the 1940 census, average Indiana sixth graders were twelve years and four months old, but in the 1970 census, they were only eleven years and six months old, nearly a full year's difference in average age. Consequently, the older 1945 students had more time in school than the "comparable" 1976 students. Further, because fewer students dropped out between ninth and tenth grade in the more recent period, the 1945 tenth grade students were, on average, higher achievers, relative to all young people their age, than were the less selective group of 1976 tenth grade students. When Farr, Fay, and Negley adjusted their results to compare "age equivalent" scores rather than "grade equivalent" scores, they found that the 1976 sample, for both sixth and tenth grade, "outscored the 1945 sample significantly on every test."

"The general national assumption that the reading abilities of our children are decreasing at an alarming rate [is] unsupported by this study," the Indiana researchers concluded. This "ungrounded alarm," however, "leads to attacks on school programs that have been developed over the same time span for which this study shows the improvement in student reading achievement."

Over the years, a few "then and now" studies have shown declining student achievement: a St. Louis Board of Education study, for example, found that reading achievement was slightly less in 1938 than it had been in 1916.[14] However, the vast majority of these reports claimed improvement, refuting widely publicized attacks on schools in each era.

Schools no longer publish such reports, perhaps because today even school officials have come to believe the generally accepted fable of school deterioration. Or perhaps they do not undertake comparative studies for good reason, because they recognize that in order to make reasonable "then and now" comparisons of test scores, they require more sophisticated controls than the informal demographic similarities noted in the earlier studies. Especially because demographic change in most districts and schools has been more rapid in recent years, "then and now" studies can no longer be taken seriously without better data on test takers' parents' education, occupation, and even income, as well as the children's race and ethnicity, family status, and other socioeconomic characteristics. These data simply do not exist to match up with past test scores, and there is no way now to create them.

Even today, there is widespread resistance, on privacy grounds, to collecting many types of background data for student test takers. Nonetheless, with increasing awareness of the importance of this kind of information, educators now often attempt to assess background characteristics of test takers. In some communities, contemporary awareness of the interaction between family characteristics and school effectiveness has led to school accountability "report cards" being grouped with and compared to report cards of schools deemed to be socioeconomically similar. But data are sometimes unreliable partly because they depend on students for reports on socioeconomic conditions of which they have little notion. Students can give notoriously poor reports of their family circumstances. They may, for instance, report that a father's occupation is "police officer" (a job increasingly held by college graduates earning middle-class incomes) when in fact the father is a night security guard (requiring not even a high school diploma and earning minimum wage). Children making reports like this are not necessarily dissembling; they simply do not understand the difference. Few schools have the resources to investigate such reports further, or the inclination to do so. Yet if there is systematic misreporting, schools may be grouped inappropriately for achievement comparisons. The problem of inaccurately reported backgrounds is clearly most serious for elementary schoolchildren, but it exists for secondary students as well.

Many education researchers use the percentage of children who receive free or subsidized meals under the federal school lunch program as a proxy for the economic status of a school. Nationally, more than half of all schoolchildren can benefit from the program. But participation rates provide only bifurcated data: a child's family is either poor enough to qualify for assistance or it is not, yet the most important distinctions between children's readiness to learn occur within each of those groups. Stable, lower-middle-class families (with incomes up to 185 percent of the poverty line, equivalent now to about $31,000 a year for a family of four) are eligible, as are welfare recipients; stable, middle-class families (earning more than about $31,000 a year) are ineligible, along with the affluent.

A more important deficiency of school lunch data is the wide range of participation, even among schools that may be socioeconomically similar. Schools often give up trying to get older children to enroll in the program; adolescents consider it "uncool." How many elementary schoolchildren enroll is also related to how aggressively school administrators and teachers promote it. Changing policy priorities of federal, state, and district officials can affect how well documented eligibility must be. In some schools, eligible children may be denied participation because applications were not properly completed; in others, ineligible children participate because of lax administration. If test scores between schools in different communities that may have the same percentage of eligible children for free or reduced-price lunches are compared, one still cannot confidently draw conclusions about relative academic effectiveness from just the data at hand.

The College Board now asks high school seniors to complete a background "Student Descriptive Questionnaire" (SDQ) before they take the SAT. Using the data from these SDQs, the College Board is able to report results like "the mean verbal score of seniors from families whose income was between $20,000 and $30,000 a year was 480 in 1997, but the mean verbal score of seniors from families whose income was between $30,000 and $40,000 a year was 496."[15] Such information is important because, even within the middle-class strata, schools have a relatively easier job educating children who are more economically secure. (The difference between families in these income brackets might, say, translate into more families being able to provide teenage children with their own bedrooms and a quieter place to do homework.) Armed with such data, a sophisticated analyst might conclude that a school in a lower-middle-class community where family income averaged less than $30,000 and whose seniors had a mean verbal SAT score of 485 was doing a better job than a school in a middle-class community where family income averaged more than $30,000 and whose seniors had a mean verbal SAT score of 490. (Education researchers would say that the first school, with lower average scores, provided more "value added" to its less advantaged student body.) But few high school students can give accurate reports of their family incomes. If the result of seniors' poor understanding of their family economic situations is that SDQs provide inaccurate information, policymakers could draw inaccurate conclusions about how well or how poorly schools are doing comparatively, or relative to the past.

Test score comparisons also are worth less because test administration is wildly inconsistent. This is a problem even for those who want to study the results of the same test given at the same time in different classrooms, schools, communities, or states. It is an incomparably greater problem when test scores are compared across decades. To take one example, it is general practice to exclude special education students and those whose home language is not English from taking standardized academic tests, either because school staff feel they are unable to adjust test conditions to accommodate disabilities, because staff feel that children may be emotionally harmed by being forced to take an inappropriate test, or because schools do not want those students' scores unfairly to affect averages. But states, and school districts within states, have very different standards for classifying such students—in one nationally standardized test in 1990, Minnesota excluded 33 percent of special education students from taking the test while Arkansas excluded 71 percent.[16]

Today, about 11 percent of the nation's students are classified as needing special education; while some have very severe emotional or physical handicaps, others have speech or hearing difficulties, mild autism, dyslexia, or other conditions that may make teaching more difficult but not excessively so. In the past, many fewer academically troubled students were diagnosed with these milder conditions; most were simply considered "slow learners" and eventually dropped out of school, some at early ages. No valid comparison of test scores can be made without knowing whether such students in earlier eras were included in each pool of test takers. And there is no way to know. For today's students, schools are required to accommodate learning disabilities by providing extra time on standardized tests, or perhaps by permitting the test to be taken on a computer. But if schools or school districts have different standards for determining eligibility for such accommodations, or differing abilities to provide them, test score comparisons can be misleading.

Some teachers may assist students in standardized test taking, while others do not. The SAT is administered in large, impersonal halls with stern, unfamiliar proctors. But almost all other "standardized" tests for which scores are reported are given in classrooms. Does a teacher walk around the class and remind a student that it is time to move on to the next section of the test? Most standardized tests are used solely for gauging overall school performance, not for evaluating individual children, and so some teachers may fail to press a student to complete (or take, or concentrate on) an exam for which there are no personal consequences.

Alternatively, does the teacher, for days or weeks before the test, abandon the regular curriculum and drill students on test-type questions, giving practice exams? Does the teacher urge the children to get a good night's sleep before the exam, or tell them there will be a class party if they do their best? According to the ETS's Robert Mislevy, the average score for a group of students can change more from varying simple conditions that may influence student motivation—like the order in which questions are presented—than from a full year of schooling.[17]

How much of a difference unmeasured background characteristics can make was illustrated by comparing and linking scores of American eighth grade students and those from other countries in the 1992 National Assessment of Educational Progress and the 1991 International Assessment of Educational Progress. It is well known that on almost any test, Japanese and Korean students tend to score higher, and in some cases much higher, than American students. The reasons for this are complex and poorly understood. But upon examining American student scores by state, one finds that average scores of students in Iowa and North Dakota are higher than average scores of students in Korea.[18] (In a recent international math and science test, the Korean average was slightly higher than the Japanese.) Is this because schools and their math instruction in Iowa and North Dakota are better than in Korea and Japan, while instruction elsewhere in America is worse? Or is it because average students in Iowa and North Dakota have more advantageous economic and social circumstances than those elsewhere in the country, or than average students in Korea and Japan? If Iowa teaching methods were used in Mississippi, would Mississippi students also have done better than Japanese students? Or would Mississippi students have to attain Iowa familial and economic characteristics for them to outscore the Japanese? Without more sophisticated data, there is no way of answering these questions with certainty, although the fact that Iowa and North Dakota have fewer poverty-stricken black and Hispanic communities than lower-scoring states is almost certainly a major part of the explanation.

4.

National Tests

The three tests that provide trend data on student achievement do not confirm the widespread belief that achievement is declining—and neither do IQ trends. The most widely publicized of these exams is the Scholastic Assessment Test (SAT), which older readers may remember calling the "Scholastic Aptitude Test." (The College Board, recognizing that there is no clear distinction between "aptitude" and "achievement," renamed the SAT the "Scholastic Assessment Test.") The other exams providing trend data are the Iowa Test of Basic Skills (ITBS) and the National Assessment of Educational Progress (NAEP).

The Scholastic Assessment Test (SAT)

SAT Trends

Concern about declining (or stagnant) quality in American education often stems from reports of average SAT scores. The SAT is the only national test for which data exist for a considerable period, although even here there are limitations to what can be known. For example, only since 1967 has the College Board reported just one score for each high school student who took the test; previously, SAT averages included not only adults who may have taken the test prior to returning to college but also multiple scores for high schoolers who took the test more than once to try to improve their performances. Following the change in 1967, the College Board has reported only the last test each student took; for purposes of evaluating the condition of American education, however, it would be more useful to know the average of the first test each senior took, as this would more closely reflect the quality of high school education, not the efficacy of SAT cram courses.[1]

Though the College Board reports the "most recent" results for what it calls "college bound seniors," in reality, many of the scores are from students whose most recent test (and thus the one included) was taken prior to the senior year. This is because any College Board annual report will include scores of juniors who will not take the test again as seniors until after the report has been published. In 1997, for example, almost one-third of the reported scores are those of juniors, not seniors. The average scores of the juniors are considerably higher than those of the seniors,[2] presumably because those who take the test as juniors are the most able students, qualified to apply to the most competitive colleges (perhaps for early admission), many of them planning to take the test again in their senior years. For earlier years, however, the College Board provides no data on the number of college-bound "seniors" included in the averages who were, in fact, not seniors at all. Because there is no way to adjust average SAT scores for the number of juniors in the pool, interpretation of published score trends is suspect.

The SAT is administered by strict proctors under carefully controlled conditions. The Educational Testing Service protects the security and reliability of the SAT by changing the test regularly, eliminating obsolete questions, mixing versions of the test that are given, and "equating" each version of the test with previous ones. (By inserting questions from previous tests into current exams, ETS can adjust scoring so students who achieved a particular score on the earlier tests achieve a comparable score on the current test).

From 1941, when the SAT in its present form was first given, to 1980, combined (verbal and math) average scores dropped from 1000 to 890. The decline was more dramatic for verbal skills (500 to 424) than for math (500 to 466).[3]

The averages dropped initially from 1000 in 1941 to 970 in 1952, held mostly steady—going up some years and down in others—until 1963, when the average was 980, and then began a steady decline to 890 in 1980. After 1980, scores rose a little bit, to 906 in 1985; for the past decade they have again been mostly unchanged, going up a little in some years and down in others. In 1997 the average score was 915,[4] considerably below the lower limit of its range in the mid-1960s.

The average has remained reasonably steady in the past ten years because declines in verbal scores have been offset by better performance in math. Indeed, mean math scores are now approaching the high point recorded in the 1960s. In 1997 the verbal average was 428, compared to 478 in 1963 (and 466 in 1967, the first year only one score was reported for each test taker); in 1997 the math average was 487, compared to 502 in 1963 (and 492 in 1967).[5]

These data are regularly interpreted in the press and by some policymakers as indicating that the quality of schooling has declined. Yet declines in SAT scores are misleading. The SAT is the worst possible test by which to evaluate the performance of American schools because it is voluntary. And if communities are especially concerned about how well elementary and secondary schools teach students who are headed for the workforce, junior colleges, or vocational schools after high school graduation, it is foolish to address this concern with a test that is designed to exclude students not planning to attend four-year academic colleges.

If a test is to be considered a valid indicator of the performance of a group of students, scores must be counted either from all students in the group or from a statistically representative selection of those students. If groups of students are to be compared from year to year, procedures in each year must be carefully controlled to make certain that the standards by which the representativeness of the sample is determined do not change. Year-on-year comparisons of groups of students will be seriously flawed if they are based on those who happened to volunteer to take the test.

Students choose to take the SAT, and to pay the fee as often as they take it, because they plan to apply to colleges that require it. But throughout most of the period that the SAT has been given, only a small percentage of American high school seniors have gone on to academic colleges, and a smaller percentage still went on to colleges that required the SAT for admission. (Many colleges, for example, require a different test, the ACT, given by the American College Testing program.) Clearly, if only the best-prepared seventeen-year-olds take the SAT the average score will be higher than if less able students took it.

One of the more egregious perversions of SAT scores has been to use these data to compare state education systems. If (as is the case in fact) only academically elite colleges in some states require the SAT but in other states all colleges require it, SAT average scores in the first group of states will be higher than in the second, though the second group of states might have superior elementary and secondary schools. If economic or social conditions inspire more students to take the test, average scores will decline even though the quality of schools actually may be improving. Conversely, school quality could be worse but SAT average scores higher in a year when a more select group of seniors took the test, perhaps because a recession caused more lower-middle-income students to defer their college plans. If Americans want to raise the nation's SAT scores, they do not need to improve schools. They can do so simply by discouraging any but the top students in every high school class from taking the test.

(Lest one think this idea far-fetched, the South Carolina legislature, concerned with bad publicity the state was receiving for having the lowest average SAT scores in the nation, considered a 1993 bill to prohibit less academically advanced students from taking the test. "We are trying to get higher SAT scores," the bill's sponsor announced. The bill did not pass.)[6]

In 1983, the Department of Education called the first of a series of annual press conferences to display a "wall chart" containing, among other statistics, average SAT scores by state.[7] School critics used these data to show that American schools were wasting money because the states whose per pupil education expenditures were the lowest were often also those with the highest average SAT scores. This linkage of SAT scores to per pupil expenditures became a rallying point for school critics. A table published on the editorial page of the *Wall Street Journal* noted that Utah spends less per pupil than any other state but has the fourth-highest SAT scores. The highest average SAT scores were posted by Iowa, though Iowa spent only half as much per pupil as New York or New Jersey, whose students' average scores were forty-second and thirty-ninth, respectively. Thus, the *Journal* concluded, Utah and Iowa schools must be more productive than schools in New York and New Jersey.

Howard Wainer, ETS's principal research scientist, reacted by saying that such reasoning is "almost surely specious"[8] because less than 5 percent of all high school seniors in Utah and in Iowa took the SAT in 1993. Most colleges in those states, and most colleges to which their high school students apply, require the ACT, not the SAT. Students in Iowa and Utah who take the SAT are usually the best students who apply to more selective colleges in the East. Or they are wealthier students who are able to afford to attend college in regions far from home where SAT requirements are more common. In New York, on the other hand, where the SAT is required by almost all colleges, 74 percent of high school seniors took it in 1993; in New Jersey it was 76 percent; in Connecticut, 78 percent.[9] The *Journal* and the wall charts, therefore, compared the top 3 percent of Utah's seniors to the top 74 percent of New York's. That the average scores of the New York and New Jersey seniors were low compared with those from Utah and Iowa tells us nothing about the quality of schools in those states or about the efficacy of spending on education.

Criticizing these attempts to draw conclusions about relative student performance from SAT data, Wainer noted:

> If we chose the top 3% from the Connecticut SAT-takers, their average scores would smother the currently top-ranked Hawkeyes. Are the 3% of Iowan high school seniors who take the SAT the best that Iowa has to offer? Who knows? We have no evidence. What would Iowa's rank be if 78% of its students took the test? Almost surely lower, but how much so? It is clear that examining the raw ranks will not get us anywhere. There have been many attempts to adjust these ranks statistically [i.e., make valid comparisons of SAT scores between states] but none were successful.[10]

Changes in SAT scores over time, for which the representativeness of test takers is also uncontrolled, similarly cannot lead to any valid deductions being made.

In its present form, the SAT was first administered to 10,654 high school seniors in April 1941. These test takers represented less than one-half of 1 percent of all seventeen-year-olds.[11] (Because half of American youth dropped out before completing high school at that time, these 10,564 students were almost 1 percent of graduating seniors.)[12] Verbal and math scores from 1941 and 1942 were ranked and "scaled": the average score was defined as being 500, and the standard deviation defined as 100; that is, the score of a student who did better than about five-sixths of fellow test takers was defined as 600, and the score of a student who only did better than only about one-sixth of his peers was defined as 400.

From 1941 to 1996, scores were calculated by comparing the number of correct answers on the SAT of each student taking the test to the number of correct answers of students who took the test in 1941. A 1980 student, for example, who did as well as the average test taker in 1941 received a score of 500; a 1980 student who got more right answers than five-sixths of 1941 test takers received a score of 600; and so on.

This system of scaled scores can be used to evaluate the performance of schools in different periods, as long as the samples of students in the different periods are comparable in profile. The College Board, however, kept no records of who took the test in 1941 and published no statistics concerning the scores of different types of students. Education researcher Gerald Bracey reports that he interviewed a former Educational Testing Service official from that period who estimated that in 1941 almost the only students who took the SAT were males, many of whom attended private prep schools, planning to attend Ivy League schools.

To understand the comparisons that could be made with good demographic data, let us play with two imaginary conditions. First, make the wild assumption that these 10,654 students were the highest achievers in their national cohort of seventeen-year-olds. Further assume that as the pool of test takers expanded from less than half of 1 percent of seventeen-year-olds in 1941 to about 30 percent in 1997,[13] each year the additional test takers came first from the second-highest-achieving group, then from the next-highest-achieving, and so on, until in 1997 the 30 percent who took the test were the most talented 30 percent of the cohort. These (entirely unfounded) assumptions would allow the average score of 1941 test takers to be measured against the average score of the top 19,000 test takers in 1997, 19,000 being equivalent to one-half of 1 percent of all seventeen-year-olds that year, or 1.7 percent of 1997 SAT test takers. In 1997 about 19,000 students scored above 750 on the math portion of the SAT, while about 18,000 scored above 690 on the verbal portion.[14] Such a comparison would show that the average SAT score of the top one-half of 1 percent of seventeen-year-olds in 1997 was considerably higher than the average SAT score of the top one-half of 1 percent of seventeen-year-olds in 1941, though the average scores in 1997 (428 on the verbal and 487 on the math) were considerably lower than the averages of 500 on each test in 1941. Similar comparisons could be made using other years, leading to similar conclusions.

Though such comparisons suggest that, contrary to popular myth, SAT score trends indicate schools provide better educations today than they did at any time since 1941, in reality this speculation has little value because it cannot be assumed that the 10,654 students who took the test in 1941 were the brightest seventeen-year-olds in the country at that time. One can reasonably assume that they were among the richest, but not necessarily the smartest. A young man who attended Exeter Academy in 1941 and who took the SAT prior to entering Harvard or Princeton was not necessarily more clever than a young man or woman who attended a public school in California and who was not then required to take the SAT prior to attending Berkeley. It is likely, of course, that the expansion of standardized test taking over the past half century represents, to some extent, a deeper dip into the talent pool, as well as down the social class structure. SAT results today are more variable than those of half a century ago: since 1972, the College Board has reported "standard deviations" of test scores, and these are greater than they were in 1941, meaning that fewer scores are grouped close to the average. But this could be attributable either to the wider range of quality now in American schools from which test takers come or to the more heterogeneous backgrounds of SAT test takers. Without knowing to what extent the growing number of test takers is attributable to an expanding academic pool or to heightened social mobility or diversity, education specialists can draw no conclusions about how changes in SAT scores reflect improvement, or lack of it, in American public schools.

Alternatively, imagine a second set of assumptions, perhaps more realistic than the first. In 1997 test takers who reported coming from homes with annual family income in excess of $100,000 had average verbal scores of about 483 and average math scores of about 555, a combined score of 1039.[15] In 1997 this group included 111,252 students. Making the very rough assumption that this group of students came from families to some extent similar in character to the families of the 10,654 test takers in 1941 (families with incomes higher than $9,268, an amount equivalent in 1997 dollars to $100,000)[16] would lead to the conclusion that students from the most economically privileged families today are considerably better prepared quantitatively, and slightly less well prepared verbally, than equivalent students in 1941—with an overall score advantage of 1039 to 1000. Obviously, the limitation is that there is no way of determining with certainty what the economic circumstances of 1941 test takers were. They were surely among the privileged, but whether they were directly comparable to children of today's families with incomes over $100,000 is not known.

The Wirtz Panel

These problems of SAT analysis are familiar to education specialists, who generally believe that about half the decline in SAT scores from the mid-1960s to the late 1970s is attributable to the shifting composition of test takers. The experts attribute the other half, however, to declining school quality or to changes in American culture (more television watching, for example) that lead to poorer student achievement. This interpretation stems from a 1977 report by a group headed by Willard Wirtz, labor secretary in the Kennedy and Johnson administrations. But Wirtz's report was more complex than its conclusion suggests. A careful reading of this influential document forces us to acknowledge that no one really knows how much the decline stemmed from social composition and how much (if any) from declining school quality.

In 1975, amidst growing concern about declining average SAT scores (dropping from 980 in 1963 to 910), the College Board appointed an "Advisory Panel on the Scholastic Aptitude Test Score Decline" to investigate. Chaired by Wirtz, it included vice chairman Harold Howe II (former U.S. commissioner of education) and nineteen other scholars and educators. How the panel came to its "50/50" conclusion illustrates how difficult it is to make informed judgments about apparent test score trends.

Wirtz's panel initially concluded that the problem was even worse than it seemed. Panel staff administered both the 1973 and 1963 SAT tests to a sample of high school seniors and found that the group did slightly better on the 1973 exam than on the 1963 exam. Thus, the panel reasoned, the 1973 test was slightly easier, and the decade-long score decline would actually be about 10 points greater if a test as difficult as the 1963 SAT were still being used.[17]

But the panel also recognized that the broadening base of SAT test takers, and the voluntary nature of the test, played some role in creating a false impression of declining school quality. The problem was to determine how much of the apparent decline simply reflected increased numbers of test takers from lower ability groups and how much could be blamed on educational failings. To apportion these causes, the advisory panel examined two other federally financed tests given to representative samples of high school seniors—Project Talent (1960–63) and the National Longitudinal Study of the Class of 1972. The panel reasoned that, to the extent SAT scores had fallen faster than reading scores from more representative tests, the drop should be attributed to the self-selection aspect of SAT test taking, not to a decline in the quality of schooling. The panel calculated that SAT scores fell about twice as much as the reading scores of all high school seniors[18] and estimated that from 1963 to about 1970, from two-thirds to three-quarters of the drop in SAT scores was attributable simply to the expanding pool of SAT test takers.[19] In addition, the panel noted, there were further unmeasurable sources of score declines in this period. As the number of SAT test takers expanded to include seniors who were planning to attend less competitive and nonelite colleges (in 1960, 350 colleges required the SAT; by 1969, 850 did so),[20] the number of seniors who took the SAT more than once began to decline. Because test repeaters usually score from fifteen to thirty points higher the second time they take the test (and because the College Board reports scores of students the last time they take the test), a smaller percentage of repeaters would also cause the average score to decline.[21]

By examining individual data on Project Talent and National Longitudinal Study subjects who had also taken the SAT, the advisory panel was able to confirm that there had been big changes from the early 1960s to the early 1970s in the percentage of SAT test takers who were from minority groups, who came from lower-income families, or who were women (women had traditionally scored lower on the math portion of the SAT).

Beginning in 1972, the College Board collected its own data on test takers, asking about family income, race and ethnicity, postcollege career plans, high school class rank, and so forth. The advisory panel deduced, based on Student Descriptive Questionnaire responses, that there had been little further change in test takers' social characteristics from 1972 to 1977, although it observed a significant increase in those who stated an intention to pursue "occupational" or "career" majors, as opposed to arts and sciences;[22] this could reflect the presence of more test takers from lower socioeconomic groups. But the ethnic composition of test takers changed slowly: black students, for example, were 7 percent of all test takers in 1973 and 8.8 percent in 1977.[23] Thus, the panel said, probably only about 20 to 30 percent of the SAT score decline in the 1973 to 1977 period was due to further changes in the make-up of the test-taking group.[24]

Overall, then, the advisory panel reasoned that about half of the SAT score decline from 1963 to 1977 must be attributable to declining school quality and other "real" factors.[25] The panel noted an increase in less serious high school elective courses, less emphasis on writing, lower standards (grade inflation, automatic promotion, less homework), watered-down textbooks (more pictures, less text), aggravating social trends (increased divorce rates and mothers working outside the home), too much television watching, and national demoralization and disillusionment (from the Kennedy and King assassinations and the Vietnam War).[26] All of these were probably responsible, according to the panel, for some unmeasurable portion of the decline.

The Wirtz panel relied for much of its data on a study by a team of College Board researchers, led by Albert Beaton, for its conclusion that about half the score decline was attributable to poorer schools. But a little-noticed appendix to Beaton's memorandum acknowledged a serious flaw. Beaton figured that educational quality had declined because average scores for all seniors had dropped from 1960 to 1972 (based on analysis of Project Talent and the National Longitudinal Study). But in this period, a declining dropout rate meant that more of the seventeen-year-old cohort remained in school, became seniors, and took the national reading tests on which Beaton's conclusions were based. If, as seems reasonable, many of those who dropped out in the earlier years were the less able students, then the decline in average reading scores for all seniors could also represent simply a change in the composition of test takers. If dropouts were, on the whole, less academically accomplished than those who completed school, it was impossible to know how much of the score decline itself was attributable to a change in educational quality—unless the test could have been given to all seventeen-year-olds, not only those remaining in school.

In 1960 high school graduates made up 69.5 percent of the seventeen-year-old population; in 1972 they were 75.6 percent.[27] Examining reading scores in a single school district, Beaton estimated that 60 percent of the decline in average reading scores of all seniors could be accounted for simply by the reduced dropout rate from 1960 to 1972.[28] "Further research is needed to determine whether this estimate would be confirmed by a formal study," he stated.[29]

The Wirtz panel judged that about half the 1963 to 1977 decline in SAT scores was owed to a deterioration of schools or of child-rearing practices. But if 60 percent of the decline attributed to this deterioration from 1963 to 1972 is in fact only a statistical consequence of a reduced dropout rate, then compositional changes explain not half but more than two-thirds of the SAT score decline from 1963 to 1977. This modified conclusion, however, is so speculative (because so little is known about changes in student demographic characteristics) that the true decline attributable to schools or cultural influences could be no more than one-third or still less. There is simply no way to know.[30]

Thus, despite the fanfare accompanying each year's release of SAT results, and the use school critics make of the data to support claims that educational quality has declined, no such conclusions can legitimately be drawn. Because so much about the characteristics of test takers is a mystery, declining or rising SAT scores could be consistent either with school improvement or school deterioration.

SAT Recentering

In 1996, concerned by the misuse to which SAT scores have been put in debates about public education, the College Board "recentered" the scale on which SAT scores are reported. Instead of calculating scores with reference to the average performance of 1941 test takers, the new scale defines average 1990 achievement as being 500. On the new scale, a 600 score now means the test taker did better than about five-sixths of test takers in 1990, not in 1941.

Because recentering disguises a favored weapon of today's public school critics, reactions have been fierce. Diane Ravitch, a historian who became assistant secretary of education in the Bush administration, charged the College Board "has turned deplorable performance on the verbal test into a new norm. The old average," she claimed, "was a standard that American education aspired to meet; the new average validates mediocrity."[31] Ravitch believes that setting a high standard for American students will help to motivate their achievement. She would be correct if the SAT were mainly a motivational device; in that case the old scale might retain value. But if students and their schools are to be judged deficient by comparing SAT scores to those of the past, then the old scale becomes not a goal but a club. Many students will forever be thought failures if the standard to which they are held is that of privileged 1941 Ivy Leaguers.

Recentering is sensible because it enables students who take the SAT to know how they compare to the "average" SAT test taker. The alternative would be for the SAT to adopt a scoring system based on well-defined and -described competencies—for example, if a 500 score on math signified not whatever the mean of a self-selected group of college-bound students in 1941 or in 1990 happened to know but the ability to perform and explain certain algebraic operations. If the SAT were scored in this "criterion-referenced" fashion, then each student cohort could reasonably be compared. However, formulating a scoring system of this sort is extraordinarily difficult. The Department of Education has attempted to develop such a scale for the National Assessment of Educational Progress, with questionable results. One reason for the difficulty is that students do not arrange themselves in a neat, linear order of competence. A criterion-referenced SAT scoring system might assume that students will progress from algebraic competence to the ability to do calculus. But some students will score well on calculus while getting algebra questions wrong.

Over the long run, the new, 1990-normed SAT scale will itself become obsolete because characteristics of students who take the test change further or because schools improve or deteriorate. The clear disadvantage of recentering is that it becomes more difficult to compare today's SAT test takers with those of past decades. But because such comparisons were always of dubious value, and have caused much mischief, this drawback is minimal. Those interested in history can always, with the proper cautions, convert College Board SAT reports to approximate original-scale equivalents, as this report does whenever mention of SAT scores is made.

That apparent SAT score declines give a false reading about American education performance often has been reported officially, not only by the Wirtz Commission but more recently as well. This makes especially puzzling the continued use of the SAT to condemn public schools.

Sandia National Laboratories in Albuquerque produced nuclear weapons components. At the end of the cold war, it began to search for a new mission. In 1990, Secretary of Energy James Watkins assigned three Sandia "systems analysts" to examine American education. These scientists had previously worked on nuclear weapons, a subject too dangerous to approach with preconceptions. They took pride in their ability to examine facts dispassionately.

In contrast to Admiral Watkins's belief that SAT scores were dropping, the group concluded, after many months spent poring over data, that "average scores of top performers are generally increasing. . . . Evidence of decline used to justify system-wide reform is based on misinterpretations or misrepresentations of the data."[32] Because these truths seemed to conflict with a Bush administration agenda of privatizing education with vouchers that could be used at nonpublic schools, the Department of Energy declined to release the report. According to Watkins, Sandia's analysis was "a call for complacency at a time when just the opposite is required. The Department of Energy will not permit publication of the study. . . ."[33]

The Iowa Test of Basic Skills (ITBS)

Many schools use national standardized tests to assess student achievement at each grade level. Some of these tests have been around for many years; several of the "then and now" studies conducted in the first half of this century (and described in Chapter 3) were based on successive administrations of the Stanford Achievement Test, an exam series still published by Harcourt Brace.* There is fierce competition between publishers for districts and states to adopt particular tests.

These commercial exams are called "norm-referenced tests" (NRTs) because each determines the average national score for each grade level and subject and then reports scores for each student, school, or district with reference to this national norm. In other words, if a school's sixth graders are reported to read at grade level, this only means that their scores are, on average, the same as the mean reading scores of all sixth graders across the nation. Alternatively, scores may be reported in percentiles: if a school's students are said to read at the fifty-fifth percentile, this means they are generally better readers than the national average. (Of the nation's sixth graders, 45 percent read better than the average sixth grader in this school, while 55 percent do not read as

---

* The Stanford Achievement Test is also known to educators as the "SAT." To avoid confusion, wherever in this report the acronym "SAT" appears, it refers to the College Board's test, not Harcourt Brace's.

well.)[34] Each time a test publisher issues a new version (called a "form") of the exam, usually about every five years, it conducts a new study to establish a new norm.

Renorming a new test form accomplishes the same function as "recentering" the SAT: it permits students to be compared to their contemporaries rather than to students of the past. Renorming is necessary because, as curricula evolve, old norms become obsolete. People no longer want to know what percentile students attain when compared to average scores for a mix of skills no longer valued. Returning to an earlier example, no one is terribly interested in what percentile students register in terms of math performance if this figure is calculated from an average (norm) of students who have never heard of set theory.

Renorming is also needed because of demographic change. As seen in the case of the SAT, a norm established for an elite group says little about the performance of a more broadly representative mass. Similarly, if society evolves in socioeconomic character, then norms based on a nationally representative group of test takers can become irrelevant. Some critics will be quick to say that simply because there may now be more poor immigrant children in our schools, this is no excuse for lowering the definition of average. That seems reasonable at first blush. But what if the reverse happens? If the nation does a better job of solving its social problems, and there are fewer disadvantaged children in schools, should tests not be renormed so that "average" represents a higher standard of achievement?

Because commercial tests are normed on a national sample of all students, not on a self-selected group like the SAT, the disadvantages of stable norms might not be as serious. Sophisticated testing experts could at least make adjustments for changing curricula when new test forms were published, allowing for both new norms and comparability with past forms.[35] And background studies could be prepared providing information about how a group of students with the socioeconomic characteristics of prior cohorts would do on the current test. But commercial test publishers do not "equate" successive forms of their tests because there is no market for this activity. School districts and states purchase tests to measure themselves against other school districts and states, not to compare themselves with the past. The failure of commercial test publishers to equate each successive version of their tests with the previous versions means that a relatively simple tool for making conclusions about progress or decline in American education is not available to us.

Nor is it feasible to link the results of the different commercial tests, so that results from students in different places and years can be pooled and conclusions about national performance drawn. According to ETS researcher Robert Mislevy, this idea is "educational assessment's counterpart to perpetual motion machines [that] unavoidably leads to disappointment, at best, or disaster if there are stakes attached to the results."[36] Not only does each publisher emphasize different skills in its test, making linkage impossible, but there is also inadequate security in the conditions under which commercial tests are administered. "Security" problems do not arise from conscious cheating but from the same teachers administering the same tests in their own classrooms year after year. They cannot help but "teach to the test" as they become more familiar with each form; invariably, scores increase over the period that a form is used and then drop again when a new form is introduced. A West Virginia physician was examining test scores about ten years ago and noticed this phenomenon: he wrote a series of articles about the "Lake Wobegon" effect where, after a few years of administering the same form of a standardized test, educators can claim that most children are above average.[37]

Of the various standardized tests given to representative samples of American students (that is, not like the SAT), only the Iowa Test of Basic Skills (ITBS) has enjoyed sufficiently consistent administration over an extended period to support even tentative conclusions about trends in American student achievement. The ITBS is developed by faculty members at the University of Iowa and sold to states and school districts by the Houghton Mifflin Company. Eleven states, including Iowa, use the ITBS as an official (or quasi-official) state test, and numerous school districts in other states also use it. Separate tests are given in the same months of each school year to grades three to eight in reading, vocabulary, spelling, capitalization, punctuation, language usage, work study skills, math concepts, math problem solving, and computation. For most of the period since the test was first introduced in 1935, scores have been expressed in "grade equivalents," that is, a score of 8.5 in vocabulary means that the student's vocabulary is average for students who are in the fifth month of the eighth grade. Before each version of the test is administered, norms for the nation (and for Iowa specifically) are established by pretesting a nationally representative sample (and a sample representative of Iowa as well), so all students who take the test can be compared to an average student in each month of a child's school career.

If grade equivalents were simply reestablished with each new form, there would be no basis for using these test results to compare student achievement, for if the average student in the fifth month of the eighth grade had a smaller vocabulary than the average student at that point ten years earlier, an unchanged score would mask a deterioration in student ability. But the scholars at the University of Iowa, now led by Professor H. D. Hoover, also equate each new test to the previous one for Iowa students, so average scores in Iowa schools can be expressed with reference to the average Iowa student's performance in past years as well. The equating studies of the University of Iowa provide a unique database for comparing the performance of students in that state.

Using grade equivalents from 1965, Hoover reports that eighth grade reading scores rose from 7.99 in 1955 to 8.47 in 1966, dropped to 7.83 in 1977, rose to 8.30 in 1988, and have declined slightly since then to 8.21 in 1997. In math, scores rose from 7.64 in 1955 to 8.45 in 1965, declined to 7.71 in 1978, and rose once more to 8.26 in 1997. In work study skills (using maps, diagrams, and references), scores rose from 7.89 in 1955 to 8.51 in 1966, declined to 8.13 in 1977, rebounded to 8.82 in 1988, and declined again to 8.61 in 1997.

In a composite measure of all test results for the eighth grade, scores climbed from 7.80 in 1955 to 8.45 in 1965, declined to 7.82 in 1977, rose to 8.43 in 1991, and dipped to 8.32 in 1997. Thus, today's Iowa eighth graders are a half-year ahead of their 1955 counterparts in academic skills and are only about one month behind their counterparts in the peak year, 1965.

For other grade levels, results are similar. The composite score for the third grade rose from 3.02 in 1955 to a high of 3.89 in 1990; it was 3.72 in 1997. Third graders are therefore more than two-thirds of a year more academically advanced than third graders were in 1955, and are about two months behind their best-performing yearly counterparts. Fifth graders in 1997 had an average mark of 5.67, less than a month's difference from the high point of 5.71 in 1992 and still better than two months more advanced than fifth graders in 1965.[38]

Iowa, of course, is not representative of the nation as a whole. As noted previously, average Iowa eighth graders do better on international math exams even than average students in Korea and Japan, while average American eighth graders overall fare much worse. Part of the reason may be that, demographically, Iowa has changed less than many other states.

The difference for most Iowa grades between current scores and the high points of 1965–68 and 1988–92 is, in itself, small enough to be unimportant, although when the 1997 results were released, Iowa officials expressed concern that if the small but steady declines since 1990 or so were to continue, especially in the lower grades, this might reflect a deterioration in school effectiveness.[39] On the other hand, while Iowa has a more economically advantaged student population than the nation as a whole, it has recently absorbed new, unskilled immigrants in its meatpacking and service industries, and this might explain some if not all of the recent score declines.

ITBS does not collect or report data on the socioeconomic characteristics of its test takers, so no one can say for sure if Iowa's test score trends reflect a more affluent population or better school practices than the rest of the country. Education research has never identified school practices in Iowa that differ significantly from those in other states, however. There is no evidence that Iowa children use more challenging textbooks or that their teachers are better than those found elsewhere in the country. So it seems reasonable to conclude that if Iowa's ITBS trends disclose no collapse in student achievement, there is probably none to be found elsewhere, at least not one attributable to a deterioration in the quality of instruction (declining scores in some other places could, of course, be attributable to a more rapid disappearance of the family characteristics that favor student achievement). The very recent falloff witnessed in Iowa's lower grades is too small to permit confident conclusions about whether it reflects changing student characteristics or less effective schools.

The pattern of Iowa scores resembles the pattern of SAT scores in one interesting respect. In each case, there was an apparent decline after the mid-1960s, followed by a recovery, so that today scores are little different than they were thirty years ago. In 1976 a psychologist at the University of Michigan, R. B. Zajonc, proposed a theory to explain falling SAT scores at that time. Zajonc suggested—this is oversimplifying his thesis a bit—that because children from larger families get less individual attention from their parents, these children are less intellectually stimulated in their early years at home and do worse in school than children from smaller families. Thus, he reasoned, the rise and fall of test scores was mostly a function of the movement of the "baby boom" through the schools. The decline of SAT scores from the mid-1960s to the mid-1970s reflected the fact that baby boomers were at that period of time old enough to take the test. The baby boom ended about 1963, and cohorts born subsequently came from backgrounds of gradually decreasing family size. Zajonc made a prediction: average SAT scores would begin to rise again after 1980, when the first children from generally smaller families were seventeen years old.[40] And they did rise as he had predicted.

In 1986–87 Daniel Koretz at the Congressional Budget Office analyzed a broad range of standardized tests, including the ITBS, that supported the Zajonc hypothesis. Koretz noted that ITBS scores for different grades did not rise or fall in the same year. Rather, grades seemed to rise or fall as a particular cohort moved through the school system. Thus, although the data do not fit perfectly, the low point for ITBS scores for each grade tended to occur about a year before the low point for the subsequent grade (for those born at the height of the baby boom from the mid-1950s to early 1960s), and the high point for each grade tended to occur about a year before the high point for the subsequent grade (for pupils born after the boom ended in the mid-1960s).[41]

Zajonc was correct that SAT scores would increase after 1980, but the increase lasted only about six years before leveling off, an event that cannot be explained by his hypothesis. And while ITBS scores began to rise as Iowa children born after the mid-1960s moved through the schools, results from the past ten years do not seem to conform to a cohort pattern. Thus, the Zajonc hypothesis is provocative, but it further illustrates how difficult it is to separate school from family and other effects in education, and how little is still known about the causes of test score trends.

The National Assessment of Educational Progress (NAEP)

In 1969, the U.S. Department of Education began to give standardized tests in science, mathematics, reading, writing, social studies, and the arts to a representative sample of nine-, thirteen-, and seventeen-year-olds. (Each subject is tested only once every few years.)

Today's public concern with declining student achievement usually assumes that test scores began to decline in the mid-1960s. Because the NAEP did not begin until afterward, it cannot shed light on the accuracy of this perception. Nonetheless, the NAEP is a valuable tool for assessing trends since the 1970s. What these data show is a mostly stable picture (as long as student scores are not disaggregated by race or ethnicity).

NAEP scores are unique because, unlike other academic measurements, all grade levels are measured on a single scale, ranging from 0 to 500. Of course, fourth grade scores are expected to be lower than twelfth grade scores. The result is that, rather than reporting scores only in relation to other scores in the same grade, the NAEP also allows a comparison of younger children with older ones and an assessment of the progress the nation's children make from year to year.

The NAEP is given to a sample of students, and subsamples take different parts of the test, so no data on individual students are available. But the NAEP does permit us to learn not only how this year's fourth graders compare to a prior year's but also how much higher on the scale this year's eighth graders are than fourth graders were four years earlier.

In reading, the NAEP is designed so that a score of 150 should reflect an ability to follow brief, written directions. A score of 200 should reflect an ability to combine ideas and make inferences based on short, uncomplicated passages. A score of 250 should reflect an ability to make inferences and reach generalizations from passages dealing with literature, science, and social studies. A score of 300 should reflect an ability to find, understand, summarize, and explain relatively complicated information. And a score of 350 should reflect an ability to synthesize and learn from specialized and complex texts like scientific materials, literary essays, and historical documents.

The NAEP also distinguishes five levels of math scores. A score of 150 should mean that students can recognize simple situations in which addition and subtraction apply. Those at the 200 level should also know basic multiplication and division and be able to read information from charts and graphs. Students at the 250 level should be able to apply addition and subtraction skills to one-step word problems, compare information from charts and graphs, and analyze simple logical relations. Those at the 300 level should be able to perform moderately complex procedures and reasoning, like computing decimals, fractions, and percents; interpreting simple inequalities; evaluating formulas; and solving simple linear equations. Students at the 350 level should be able to solve two-step problems using variables, identify equivalent algebraic expressions, and develop an understanding of functions and coordinate systems.

When nine-year-olds were first tested in math in 1973, their average score was 219. For the next ten years, this result did not change. But since the 1986 test, nine-year-olds' mean math score has started to creep up and is now at 231. The upward movement, though small, has been consistent across all levels of ability—the average score of the highest-scoring 25 percent of nine-year-olds has gone from 256 in 1978 to 268 in 1996; for the middle 50 percent, it has gone from 221 to 232; and for the lowest-scoring 25 percent, it has gone from 178 to 191.[42]

The results are similar for thirteen- and seventeen-year-olds. The thirteen-year-olds' math average was 266 in 1973 and 274 in 1996; scores throughout the range of competencies were also mostly higher in 1996 than in earlier testing periods.[43] Seventeen-year-olds' math average was 304 in 1973, fell to 298 in 1982, but recovered to a high of 307 in 1996. In each quartile here as well, average scores were mostly higher in 1996 than in earlier test administrations.[44]

In reading also, each of the three age groups had higher scores in 1996 than when the test was first given in 1971. (As opposed to the math results, there was no dip in the early years.) And similarly, the gains were consistent in both the higher- and lower-scoring quartiles. In writing and in science, however, while scores for nine-year-olds showed a pattern like that for math and reading, scores for the higher age groups were lower in 1996 than previously.

In each case, the changes over the past twenty-five years are small but statistically significant. On the whole, they show no deterioration in overall academic performance during this period. There is no way of knowing how the academic achievement reflected by today's NAEP scores would compare with achievement prior to 1970, when the exams were first administered. However, because the pattern of NAEP scores is consistent with the pattern of ITBS scores for Iowa students during the same period, it would not be reckless to guess that results for a test like the NAEP would probably have shown stable academic proficiency for the past fifty or sixty years.

This raises a more difficult question: if scores have been stable, have they been stable at an unacceptably low level or at an adequate one? Since 1992 whenever the Department of Education has reported NAEP results, it has characterized the scores not only by numerical scale but also as "below basic," "basic," "proficient," or "advanced." The National Assessment Governing Board (NAGB), a joint public-private commission that supervises the NAEP, determines cutoff points for each of these levels. For example, the minimum "proficient" score for fourth grade math is supposed to be 245; for eighth grade math it is 295, and for twelfth grade math it is 330.[45] Different cutoffs are established for each test.

By these standards, American schools are in crisis. In reading, only 30 percent of fourth and eighth graders, and only 36 percent of twelfth graders, are "proficient." In math, only 21 percent of fourth graders, 24 percent of eighth graders, and 16 percent of twelfth graders are "proficient."[46]

Yet while score trends over time are in themselves reliable (ETS also administers the NAEP, and follows careful procedures to select samples and equate successive tests), judgments that scores "should be" higher are risky. That might be justifiable if there were a "benchmark" available, some period in the past when scores were at the level consensus determined to be satisfactory, although, as discussed above, even here the comparison could be misleading if the demographic characteristics of test takers changed over time. In this case it is probably safe to say there was never a period when all (or even many) fourth graders were "proficient" in reading and math by contemporary NAGB standards.

How then, are judgments made that an NAEP score of 245 is what should be expected of all fourth graders? These judgments are not based on history, as the NAEP has been given only for about twenty-five years. The standards also are not consistent with some other data on student achievement. For example, the NAGB standards indicate that in 1992 only 2 percent of U.S. twelfth graders had achieved an "advanced" level in mathematics. Yet, in the same year, nearly twice that number (3.8 percent) of all high school graduates were awarded college credit in calculus because they passed highly demanding advanced placement exams—designed to measure mastery not merely of the high school curriculum but also of college mathematics. Advanced placement exams are given in only a minority of U.S. high schools; if they were given to all students, more than 3.8 percent of all high school graduates might achieve passing scores.[47] Similarly, 7 percent of all high school seniors scored higher than 600 on the SAT math test in 1992,[48] a score that all observers agree reflects "advanced" math achievement; students scoring at this level would have numbered many more if the SAT had also been taken by college-bound students in states where the ACT is more common.

The NAGB standards are also not based on performance levels attained in other countries. While scores of U.S. students on international tests are generally lower than scores of their peers in other advanced industrial nations in eighth grade math, they are about the same in science,[49] and on some reading tests, American students score comparatively well. On the 1990–91 reading test administered by the International Association for the Evaluation of Educational Achievement, America's nine-year-olds scored second-highest in the world (the Finns were first).[50] But if the NAEP achievement levels established by NAGB are to be believed, only 30 percent of U.S. nine-year-olds are proficient in reading. This is simply not plausible, and it raises questions about how the proficiency levels are determined by the National Assessment Governing Board before they are broadcast to the American people in support of a "failing schools" story.

The procedure for defining these achievement levels, in reality, is both ideologically and technically suspect. The standards seem to have been established primarily for the purpose of confirming preconceptions about the poor performance of American schools. The specification of such levels is an extraordinarily complex undertaking; it would challenge even the most expert psychometricians. As became clear in the earlier discussion on how difficult it would be to set up a criterion-referenced scale for the SAT, it is not obvious how a cutoff point should be fixed that fairly reflects the fact that, although most students learn algebra before calculus, some students may do better in calculus than in algebra. Similar problems arise in all subject areas.

The National Assessment Governing Board that established these achievement levels consists of twenty-six appointees, including elected officials (for example, the governors of Illinois and Colorado), state education officials, classroom teachers, a teacher's union officer, school administrators, and two academic experts. The board in turn has appointed panels of teachers, professors, business leaders, and other citizens to decide which NAEP questions a student should be expected to answer correctly if that student is deemed to be at the basic, proficient, or advanced levels. But these panelists were given no standard by which to make these judgments. Given that even informed opinion is frighteningly detached from reality when it comes to judging what student performance was like in the past, there can be little confidence that any such panel of professionals and laypersons is capable of deciding, based solely on personal expectations, what students "should" be expected to know today.

Even if the panelists' personal opinions are accepted as valid, the procedures by which their opinions were translated into definitions of achievement levels were technically flawed. Each panelist considered what percentage of NAEP questions a "basic," "proficient," or "advanced" student should answer correctly on each test, and the percentages arrived at by all panelists were then averaged.[51] There was wide variation in the panelists' opinions, suggesting that an "average" might incorporate great subjectivity. The method also took no account of the fact that (as in the algebra-calculus continuum) some students get more difficult questions right while answering certain less difficult questions incorrectly.

In 1993, the General Accounting Office undertook a study of how these NAGB proficiency levels were established. Among its many technical findings, for example, the GAO concluded that because the method did not properly distinguish between easier and more difficult test items, students whose NAEP scores were only at the basic level actually answered correctly far more easy questions than the NAGB panelists had predicted. The same was true of students whose scores were considered proficient. Students at the advanced level, on the other hand, answered fewer difficult questions correctly than they were expected to, but pumped up their average scores by answering a higher percentage of easier questions than expected. Therefore, the GAO concluded, the cutoff scores for basic and proficient students should have been set considerably lower than they were, based on the NAGB panel's own standards, resulting in much larger numbers of students placing at these levels.[52] If the GAO is right, this calls into question not only whether the percentages of "non-proficient" students are as high as the NAEP reports suggest, but also whether the proportion of urban, poor, and minority students deemed to reach even a "basic" level of performance is as low as reported.

In response to such criticism, the Department of Education commissioned its own study of the NAGB achievement levels, undertaken by a National Academy of Education (NAE) panel. Confirming the findings of the GAO, the NAE panel concluded that the procedure by which the achievement levels had been established was "fundamentally flawed" and "subject to large biases," and that the achievement levels by which American students had been judged deficient were set "unreasonably high."[53] The National Academy of Education recommended to the Department of Education that NAEP achievement levels (as opposed to the scale scores themselves) should not be reported. In fact, the NAE panel stated, continued use of these standards could set back the cause of education reform because it would harm the credibility of the NAEP test itself.[54] The NAE's advice has not been followed.

In addition to its technical criticisms, the GAO study also attacked the NAGB standards for being implemented without proper technical review. The GAO concluded that the Department of Education went ahead with these standards anyway because "the benefits of sending an important message about U.S. students' school achievement appeared considerable, and NAGB saw little risk in publishing scores and interpretations that had yet to be fully examined. . . . NAGB viewed the selection of achievement goals as a question of social judgment that NAGB, by virtue of its broad membership base, was well suited to decide."[55] Sending a message of school failure was more important than making certain that the message was correct.

IQ Tests

In sum, neither the College Board's SAT, nor commercial tests like the ITBS, nor the Department of Education's NAEP provides serious evidence of a broad decline in American student achievement. Neither do the results of these tests, in themselves, provide any basis for conclusions that American student achievement should reasonably be higher, has ever been higher, or should be rising faster than it is today. Perhaps pupils' rates of learning ought to be accelerated, but these data provide no bases upon which such a goal can be established.

A look at IQ score patterns reinforces the points being made about the unreliability of using test results to support the claim of declining school quality. Analyses of education do not usually include IQ results because most people believe that IQ tests measure innate "ability," genetically determined, not learning. But while IQ tests are the best gauge that psychometricians have developed to measure ability, the tests are not perfect in this respect. Because all children (and adults) are products of both nature and nurture, confounded in ways no one fully understands, IQ tests tell something about acquired (as opposed to "innate") ability and about achievement as well.

IQ tests are scaled in much the same fashion as the SAT. In this case, the score of an "average" member of the population is defined as 100. A score higher than that attained by about five-sixths of the population is defined as 115, and a score higher than that of only the lowest-scoring sixth of the population is defined as 85.

Many environmental factors pollute the purity of IQ tests as measures of innate ability. Parenting styles, nutrition, family structure—indeed all the background circumstances that affect student achievement can also affect IQ test performance. For IQ tests, however, another background influence is apparently schooling itself. One confirmation of this came as a result of IQ tests administered during and after World War II in the town of Eindhoven, Holland. A Dutch psychologist, A. D. de Groot, investigated the IQs of adolescent boys in a vocational school who lost more than a year of instruction during and immediately after the Nazi occupation. De Groot found there had been a big drop in the average IQs of boys in the school from 1944 to 1947, compared with those in school from 1938 to 1943.[56] By 1951, when functioning schools had been reestablished for several years, the average IQ scores had returned to a "normal" level of 100.[57]

In the United States, another set of studies traced the IQs of black youths whose families migrated from the South to the North in the postwar period. Children who had similar grades in school in the South seemed to diverge in terms of ability after some families left in search of better prospects. Those whose families moved to northern cities tested with higher IQs than their counterparts who remained in the South. The higher IQ scores presumably resulted from attendance at superior schools in the North rather than the neglected, segregated schools of the South.

Several other studies have shown that students who stay in school longer have higher IQ scores, even though these students are identical in every measurable respect to those with less schooling.[58] So schools seemingly have something to do with IQ results, though it is not known exactly how this works or how important the effect is.

Surprisingly, average IQ scores of Americans have been rising since at least 1932. This went unnoticed for some time because, like the commercial academic achievement exams, each form of an IQ test is renormed when it is first issued. Few experts had bothered to equate successive versions of standard IQ ability tests. Psychometricians were only concerned to ensure that each version of the test was normed properly—that is, the test was constructed so that the average score would be 100 and about two-thirds of all Americans would get scores between 85 and 115. As with achievement tests, different forms of IQ tests can be equated only if a carefully selected sample of individuals is given both the current test and a previous version. A few such multiple test administrations had been conducted over the years, but for a long time it did not occur to anyone to bring them together to see whether they disclosed anything about long-term trends.

Then a New Zealand psychologist, James Flynn, collected all the cases he could find in which two or more versions of a conventional IQ test were given to the same set of subjects. He found that from 1932 to 1978, American IQs grew by fifteen points. In other words, while the average American IQ in 1978 was about 100 (by definition), if American IQs in 1978 had been assessed using 1932 IQ tests, the average would have been 115.[59] Flynn went on to discover that the same phenomenon had occurred in thirteen other industrial nations as well, where IQ gains ranged from five to twenty-five points over a similar time span.[60]

These are enormous gains. If IQ tests were a pure measure of intellect, these numbers would mean that the average American in 1978 had greater intellectual ability than five-sixths of all Americans in 1932. But clearly such IQ differences cannot possibly be explained by the hereditary traits it is popularly assumed the test measures. Even the most selective breeding among human beings could not effect such significant genetic change in so brief a period. While nobody could seriously argue that the IQ changes are attributable solely to improved (or longer) schooling, it is likely that education is one important contribution. Better nutrition, health care, or economic circumstances could also play a role, and so could the sophisticated intellectual stimulation provided by our more technologically advanced environment.

But it is quite improbable that these remarkable IQ gains (now termed the "Flynn effect" by social scientists) could have been registered if schools were decaying or even stagnant. The IQ results are one more bit of evidence that the impression of deterioration is a fable, no matter how powerfully attractive that fable may be.

5.

Improvement in the Education of Minority Students

To this point, there is no serious evidence for a decline in school quality. It is probable that the education children receive is at least as good as in any perceived golden age. More likely, it has been improving for most of this century.

But there is one respect in which less caution is needed about making a definitive statement. The academic achievement of minority youth, particularly blacks, has improved dramatically in the past quarter century. When the Coleman Report was issued in 1966, Charles Silberman wrote in a *Fortune* magazine review:

> To put the case bluntly, we simply do not know how to educate children from lower-class homes. . . . The Coleman Report makes it plain that our present efforts to help minority and lower-class youngsters are failing.[1]

Education specialists and the public at large still may not fully understand how outcomes can be secured for minority and lower-class children that are comparable to those for the more privileged, or even whether such a feat will ever be possible, but American schools have come a long way since 1966.

The Scholastic Assessment Test (SAT)

As noted earlier, in 1972 the College Board began to collect student background data for test takers; in 1976, it began to report SAT scores by race and ethnicity. The data are encouraging. For the twenty years that race and ethnic data for SAT test takers are available, average scores for all students who took the test have moved up slowly from 903 in 1976[2] to 915 in 1997.[3] In 1976, white students represented more than 75 percent of all test takers[4] and had an average score of 944.[5] In 1997, white students constituted only about 65 percent of all test takers,[6] and their average score was higher, 953.[7]

In 1976, black students were about 7 percent of all test takers[8] and had an average score of 686.[9] In 1997, black test takers represented more than 10 percent[10] of the total and had an average score of 745.[11] This is a remarkable gain not only in terms of performance but also in participation. The number of black students taking the SAT increased by 71 percent (while the pool of all test takers grew only by 13 percent) in this two-decade span. Meanwhile, the number of black seventeen-year-olds in the national population increased by only 3 percent.[12] Something was happening to make black seventeen-year-olds considerably more likely to take the test than previously.

In part, the growth in the number of black test takers may be attributable to schools' successful efforts to stimulate black students' ambitions: promising black students, whose 1976 counterparts may not have aspired to go to college, now seek higher education. But these greater ambitions may result also from forces other than school influences. A growth in the black middle class may have led more black families to feel economically secure enough to send their children to college, so that these children now take the SAT whereas comparably able children may not have bothered to do so twenty years ago.

But with so large a growth in the population of black seventeen-year-olds who take the SAT, it is also reasonable to expect that the SAT now dips deeper into the talent pool of black seniors, resulting in a greater proportion of academically less capable black students taking the SAT than was the case in 1976. Yet, despite today's presumed wider ability range among black SAT test takers, their average score has jumped substantially. It is almost certainly the case that this SAT progress reflects substantial improvement in the instruction of disadvantaged black youth.

Other influences may also have played a role, particularly the family characteristics whose impact is so intertwined with that of schools. Perhaps the most important is the documented relationship between test scores and parental educational attainment (years of school completed). Students whose parents graduated from high school can be expected to do better in school themselves. As noted previously, this may be because parents with more school experience, regardless of the quality of their education, give greater emphasis to the importance of schooling in the environments they create at home. To the extent that this is the case, the improvement of blacks' SAT scores may also result indirectly from the attempts by schools to inculcate values favorable to education among the previous generation.

Only about 39 percent of the parents of 1976 black high school seniors were likely to have been high school graduates; by 1997, about 77 percent of the parents of black high school seniors had graduated from high school. Only about 5 percent of the parents of 1976 black high school seniors were likely to have been college graduates; by 1997, this percentage had nearly tripled.[13] This is a very large single-generation gain. The substantial effort made to reduce the number of minority youths dropping out of school in the 1970s may have paid off in the higher SAT scores of black youth today. And society may not yet have realized the full benefits of this progress: black children are born today to parents 85 percent of whom have graduated from high school and 19 percent of whom are college graduates.[14]

Other minority groups have demonstrated similar advances on the SAT, although not quite of the same magnitude. The number of Mexican-origin students who took the SAT quadrupled from 1976 to 1997,[15] yet these students still experienced a gain of 18 points in average score, from 781[16] to 799.[17] Because the ranks of Mexican-American seventeen-year-olds in the total population increased only by about 31 percent in this period,[18] it is again likely that this growth in the number of test takers reflects a somewhat deeper dip into the talent pool, and once more schools can fairly claim some responsibility for the rise in scores that nonetheless occurred. When one considers that a larger proportion of the Mexican-origin seventeen-year-old population in 1997 consisted of immigrants than in 1976 (those who did not benefit from twelve years of schooling in this country), the rise in the number of test takers relative to the size of their age cohort appears even more impressive. College Board reports do not permit us to disaggregate these data by native- and foreign-born test takers.

Similarly, Puerto Rican students increased their numbers in the test taking pool by more than 200 percent, while the size of the seventeen-year-old Puerto Rican cohort grew only by 5 percent.[19] Yet Puerto Rican students still posted a gain of 27 points in average score, from 765 to 792.[20]

One interesting consequence of these trends is that the average score of each racial and ethnic group—whites, blacks, Mexican-Americans, Puerto Ricans, and others—has gone up by more than the average of all student scores. This is an example of a simple arithmetic phenomenon known as "Simpson's Paradox": if an average is composed of subgroups, it can decline while each subgroup's average increases if the number of participants in subgroups with lower averages has increased relative to those subgroups with higher averages. At various times in the past twenty years, this paradoxical situation has characterized national or state SAT score trends. Average SAT scores for minority groups started at lower points, and are still lower, than average scores for whites, although the gap is narrowing. The average SAT score of each minority group increased, as did the average score of whites; nevertheless the average score of all SAT test takers declined or stagnated because the number of minority group test takers increased relative to the number of white test takers. The failure of many school critics to understand this simple consequence of arithmetic weighting has contributed to widespread misinterpretation of SAT score reports.

Given the expectation that greater diversity of test takers would adversely affect reported average performance, both generally and within population subsets, when average scores increase simultaneously with big increases in the share of each racial and ethnic minority group taking the test, something may be happening to which it is worth paying attention. For each of these minority groups, the score pickup from 1976 to 1997 was greater on the math than on the verbal test, although in each case the verbal score increased as well. A reasonable inference would be that the dramatic rise in minority student scores is an outcome that owes something to the progressively better job that schools are doing for minority students, especially in math.

The National Assessment of Educational Progress (NAEP)

NAEP results confirm that minority students have improved their achievement substantially. In math, the average NAEP score of white seventeen-year-olds has gone up slightly over the past twenty years, from 310 in 1973 to 313 in 1996.[21] For black seventeen-year-olds, there was a bigger gain, from 270 in 1973 to 286 in 1996 (there was a high point of 289 in 1990, followed by a steady average of 286 in 1992, 1994, and 1996).[22] For Hispanic seventeen-year-olds, scores went from 277 in 1973 to 292 in 1996.[23] The scores of nine- and thirteen-year-old minority students have shown similar gains (except that in the case of thirteen-year-old Hispanics, 1996 average math scores were slightly below a peak reached in 1992).[24]

Thus, the gap between whites' and minorities' test scores narrowed. In 1973, the average black seventeen-year-old's math NAEP score was forty points lower than the average white's score. By 1990, the gap had been reduced to about twenty-two points.[25] In 1978, the average black seventeen-year-old scored better than only about 14 percent of white students in math; twelve years later, in 1990, the corresponding figure was 25 percent.[26] On the reading test, the black-white gap for seventeen-year-olds was reduced from fifty-two points in 1971 to thirty points in 1990. In 1980, the average black seventeen-year-old scored better on the reading test than 10 percent of white students; ten years later, that statistic had climbed to 22 percent.[27] These are big gains for such a short period of time.

Since 1990, it seems that the gap between white and minority academic achievement on the NAEP has stopped narrowing. However, the patterns of performance are uneven, and it is too soon to draw conclusions about such complex and recent data. For example, the black-white gap in NAEP seventeen-year-olds' reading scores was 53 points in 1971 (239 versus 291; figures are rounded off), steadily narrowed to 20 points in 1988 (274 versus 295), widened to 37 points in 1992 (261 versus 297), and since then has again narrowed, to 29 points in 1996 (265 versus 294).[28] For nine-year-olds, recent trends are similar: narrowing gaps from 1971 to 1988, then a widening, then a new narrowing, so that the gap today is about as small as at the minimum point in 1988. For thirteen-year-olds, the narrowest gap was also attained in 1988; a subsequent widening has been halted, and the gap is now about the same as it was in 1988.[29]

On the SAT, the minority-white gap has widened a little bit since 1988, not because minority scores have been declining but because white scores (particularly in math) have moved up more rapidly in the past few years. While blacks' and Puerto Ricans' scores have continued to increase over the past decade, Mexican-American student scores have declined slightly; however, the number of Mexican-American test takers has jumped by 75 percent in the past ten years alone, so the slight decrease in scores over this period may well be consistent with substantially improved achievement.

How should these gains be interpreted? Superficially, they do not seem to provide support for the fable of a collapsing urban school system, but can schools take any credit for improved minority test scores? Or are these the result of changes in family characteristics like more educationally oriented home environments?

NAEP collects very inadequate background data on test takers. Besides reporting scores by three race/ethnic groups (white, black, and Hispanic), NAEP provides additional breakdowns of score data by type of community: "advantaged urban," "disadvantaged urban," "extreme rural," and "other," and no cross-tabulations between the race/ethnic and the community categorizations are reported. To overcome the limitations of these NAEP results, RAND research scientist David Grissmer developed a procedure for estimating the extent to which these score gains have resulted from students' family characteristics. He began by analyzing two other sets of tests, each given once to adolescents in the 1980s: the National Longitudinal Survey of Youth (NLSY) and the National Education Longitudinal Study (NELS). Students who took these tests were surveyed in greater detail about their family incomes, the number of parents living at home, the number of siblings, and their parents' educational attainment (years of school completed), race, and ethnicity. Matching these background data with student test results, Grissmer was able confirm the well-known proposition that family characteristics are statistically related to scores; he was able to specify how much lower test scores were likely to be for students from poorer families or for students whose parents were less educated than the average. Grissmer's statistics did not show that a poor student was doomed to be uncompetitive; some poor students do get higher test scores than many rich ones. What he did show, however, was that in both the NLSY and NELS the distribution of scores varied dependably for students with different family characteristics when other factors were equal.

Noting that there have been great changes in students' family situations since 1970, Grissmer utilized the relationships between scores and student backgrounds in the NLSY and NELS to investigate NAEP results and to calculate what NAEP scores would have been if students' family characteristics were different. Specifically, examining students who took the NAEP test in the early 1970s, he determined what their scores would have been if these students possessed the family characteristics that Census records showed students actually had in 1990 (but had retained the educations they actually received in schools in the 1960s and 1970s). And he could then compare these imputed NAEP scores to those actually recorded.

Most people would probably expect that these "predicted" scores would be lower. This is what Grissmer initially expected to find: after all, today there are more single-parent families and more poverty than in 1970, so achievement ought to be lower. But, on the contrary, Grissmer found that when he pretended 1970s students had 1990 family characteristics, their scores jumped to higher levels than were actually obtained on the NAEP tests. Predicted scores were higher because while some family traits evolved in ways that adversely affected student achievement, others developed in the opposite direction. In particular, parental education levels increased in the most recent generation, and family size decreased. As noted, black students taking tests in the 1990s come from families where parents have considerably more education than had the parents of black students who took tests in the 1970s. According to Grissmer's calculations, a child whose parents graduated from college is likely, all other things being equal, to have a NAEP score that is eighteen points higher in percentile terms than a child whose parents did not graduate from high school.[30]

More parental education means children get more academic support at home; smaller family size means they get more parental attention. These attributes, which tend to produce higher scores, strengthened more than enough to cancel the negative influences. For example, average family income for all families was unchanged (after adjustment for inflation) from 1970 to 1990, while poverty actually became more prevalent. But because of smaller family sizes, average income per child still increased in this period. So changing family characteristics should have produced higher, not lower, scores for these imaginary 1970 students with 1990 family characteristics. Put another way, if actual 1990 students had gone to schools identical to those that 1970s students attended, the predicted NAEP scores of these 1990 students would still have been higher than those of the 1970 students.

Grissmer next looked at actual NAEP scores in the early 1990s and compared these to his predicted scores. This enabled him to determine what part of the actual changes in NAEP scores from the early 1970s to the early 1990s was a result of changes in students' family characteristics and what part could be attributed to other sources like changes in school effectiveness.[31] Overall, average NAEP test scores did creep up in this twenty-year period, as Grissmer's demographic theory predicted they should, even if schools were no better in 1990 than they were in 1970. Minority NAEP scores rose more than the average, and they rose more than did those of white students.

Grissmer estimated that the gap between whites' and blacks' math and reading NAEP scores was reduced by about 40 percent from 1975 to 1990.[32] Whites' test scores, he calculated, went up by about as much as white students' improved social and economic circumstances should have led one to expect. (This was a very slight improvement.) But black students' reading and math scores improved by more than twice the predicted amount, that is, twice what the demographics alone can explain.[33] For all minority students, math test scores jumped three times as much as could be expected purely on the basis of demographic changes.[34]

In the past generation, funding for compensatory and bilingual education programs has grown faster than funding for regular education. Could this have caused the results Grissmer documented? No one can know for sure because while Grissmer showed that family characteristics cannot alone explain the relatively faster improvement of minority student achievement, his statistical analysis provides no evidence for evaluating what else has made a difference. It is possible that other, non-measured changes have produced the minority test score surge. The very recent (1988 to 1996) pattern of short-term reversals followed by recovery could be consistent with less and then more effective schools, or it could be consistent with more effective schools combined with family and community characteristics that have varied in favorability. Data simply do not exist to draw reliable conclusions on these very recent trends. All that can be said for sure is that, like SAT score trends, NAEP trends provide no support for the notion of declining school achievement, particularly where minority students are concerned.

There is another set of data that suggests a more optimistic picture than people are generally wont to believe. There is a narrowing gap between average IQ scores of black and white youth.[35] Historically, this gap was about fifteen points, but it is now closer to ten. In other words, while the entire population's IQ scores have increased by about fifteen points during the past fifty years (the "Flynn effect" discussed in the previous chapter), the gain for blacks has been even greater. As with the other indicators of a narrowing black-white performance gap, it is unknown to what extent school effectiveness is a cause of this trend but it seems probable that schooling plays a part.

There is, of course, a wide variation in school quality, and there are seriously dysfunctional schools in many impoverished minority communities. These are mostly (but not always) schools where the overwhelming social and economic problems children bring to class lead teachers and administrators to set their goals too low. In some of these schools, problems of drugs and violence force learning to take a low priority. In others, poor housing and unstable incomes cause children to move from school to school so often that no teacher can take coherent responsibility for their instruction. And in others, facilities are so decrepit that they reinforce an expectation of failure. Anecdotal reports about these schools are accurate, but, misused, they can create a false impression that this is typical of all schools minority children attend, camouflaging the broad statistical trends about the dramatic, though not yet sufficient, improvement in minority student achievement. As black and Hispanic middle-class populations have grown, families have moved from the inner cities to the suburbs the way middle-class families long have done. The highly publicized troubled schools serve only the most disadvantaged children who remain in the urban core, while the statistical reports of improved test results may reflect mostly the capabilities of more advantaged minority youth.

But the anecdotes are misleading as well because there is a growing number of impressively successful inner city schools whose achievements are less widely appreciated. The *Education Week* special report on the "urban challenge," mentioned in the introduction, not only described Cleveland as a "study in crisis," in which students' social and economic difficulties have overwhelmed the school system's ability to educate; it also described El Paso, the fifth-poorest metropolis in the nation, where 60 percent of Hispanic students and 56 percent of black students pass Texas's minimum proficiency exam, and where 95 percent of all ninth graders take algebra and 58 percent pass it.[36]

Nor is El Paso unique. In Milwaukee, 87 percent of the city's 1996 black high school graduates passed a tough mathematics proficiency test before getting their diplomas. In Providence, 97 percent of black ninth graders were enrolled in algebra in 1994.[37] It may still be the case that the dysfunctional schools in the nation's poorest minority communities far outnumber the successful ones. The positive trends for minority students overall may primarily result from middle-class suburbanization. But to allow unsystematic, anecdotal accounts of some failing inner-city schools to color our assessment of broader progress in American education generally, and for minority students in particular, would certainly be to miss a very important part of the story.

6.

Getting Back to Basics

Many proponents of the idea that school effectiveness has declined, particularly for lower-achieving minority students, think they understand the source of this presumed failure. The culprit is modern methods that deviate from pedagogies with established records of success. Phonics as a way to teach reading has been abandoned, standards have been diluted because students who have not mastered the curriculum are routinely promoted, and a minority, "separatist" agenda reflects contempt for schools' historic assimilationist mission by ignoring the importance of teaching English to immigrant children.

But in each case, these simplistic diagnoses provide no useful guidance about how minority student achievement might be further improved. Furthermore, each of these critiques is based on myths rather than the record. Phonics, retention of failing students at grade level, and English immersion are not "traditional." They were either never tried in the absolute form their advocates now promote, or they were abandoned generations ago for the same reasons educators resist them today. Invented nostalgia for these methods is part of a broader fiction that literacy and numeracy once flourished in American schools, along with test scores at higher levels than today.

LEARNING TO READ WITH PHONICS

Phonics: The Controversy

About 80 percent of American parents, according to polls, blame young people's reading problems on a failure to teach "phonics," the process of learning the sounds that each letter symbolizes and combining these sounds to make words. Phonics, says a 1996 *Wall Street Journal* article, is the "traditional method, . . . the way baby boomers and their own parents learned to read."[1]

The importance of phonics seems intuitively obvious to most laypersons. But if phonics drills are essential to reading proficiency, how is it that Chinese and Japanese children seem so well educated? Their languages consist not of letters denoting sounds but of "characters," pictures symbolizing whole words. Chinese children memorize these symbols, and when they read, they cannot sound out a word they do not remember; their written language has no sounds. Educated adults know about five thousand characters.[2] In Japan, only two thousand characters (called kanji) are essential for basic literacy. Still, Japanese children memorize 76 kanji in the first grade, 145 in the second grade, 195 in the third grade, and so on, gradually memorizing more each year as reading becomes more sophisticated.[3] Japan has now developed a phonetic language ("hiragana") as a backup, but children must still memorize word symbols to read literature, a newspaper, or routine business correspondence.

It is not only the Chinese and Japanese who memorize picture-symbols: every reader of this page does so by recognizing whole words. If you stopped to sound out the words in this book, you would consume many days reading it and would often forget the point of a sentence before it was completed. No proficient reader of English actually uses phonics to decode it. Rather, they, like the Chinese and Japanese, learn to recognize entire words, even phrases and sentences, at a glance. The more proficient the reader, the less attention paid to individual words and syllables.

Should American children *first* learn to sound out a word before they commit it to memory? In languages like English, phonics seems a reasonable way to sound out new words, although it is not fully reliable because English phonics rules are complex, with many exceptions. But even if phonics is sometimes useful for sounding out new or unfamiliar words, it may not be the only, or even the best, way good readers learn to read.

Chapter 4 noted that on a reading test given to nine-year-old children from thirty-two countries, the best readers were Finns. Yet while Finnish is more regularly phonetic than English, teachers in Finland do not rely exclusively on phonics to teach reading.[4] Because their country is small and their language unique, Finnish children grow up watching foreign television programs in other languages. If Finnish children want to understand their Saturday morning cartoons, they must learn to read Finnish subtitles. As dialogue flashes across the screen, children have no time to sound out words. Rather, they come to recognize words and phrases by seeing them in context, associated with visual images. Indeed, Finnish children's reading improves the more television they watch, up to about three and a half hours a day.[5] Learning to read is apparently more complicated than combining sound symbols.

Phonics: The History

Conventional wisdom now proclaims that phonics was the preferred and successful method of teaching reading until fuzzy-thinking educators seized control of American schools during the past quarter century. But, contrary to the *Wall Street Journal*'s claim, baby boomers and their parents did not learn to read mostly with phonics. Many learned with books like the "Dick and Jane" series, based on a "whole word" or "look-say" approach. These readers repeated a few words endlessly until they became so familiar that a child could recognize them instantly. ("Run, Dick, run. Run, run, run. See Dick run.") New words were introduced slowly and repeated until they became familiar. The pedagogy was strikingly similar to the Japanese strategy, in which characters to be learned each year are specified in the curriculum. In the 1950s, most American reading textbooks expected children to recognize about a thousand words by the end of the second grade and another three hundred or so in the third grade[6] (a somewhat faster pace than kanji mastering in Japan). The books were dull because the method did not permit introduction of new words if they were not on the prescribed memorization list for a particular age and reading level. The approach preferred by many educators today, "whole language" (as opposed to "whole word") is a reaction to this numbing boredom. Whole language instruction attempts to make reading more interesting by giving children books with larger vocabularies, encouraging guesses at the meaning of words not yet memorized.

Whole word instruction was the preferred American method from about 1920 to 1935, although actual practice varied enormously from district to district and perhaps from teacher to teacher. Despite the preference of experts for whole word instruction, phonics probably received more emphasis in classrooms than reading specialists recommended. From about 1935 to 1970, whole word instruction was supplemented by some phonics, whereby children were taught sounds of letters by analyzing words already learned by sight.[7] So it is unlikely that many of today's school critics themselves learned to read with the phonics they now insist is the only successful approach.

Phonics was given more emphasis during the 1970s, but in the 1980s whole language gained currency.[8] In 1990, American nine-year-olds whose reading instruction had been heavily influenced by whole language theory scored second in the world on the international reading exam where Finns finished first. American fourteen-year-olds, who had begun to read when phonics was being given more emphasis, scored ninth in the world with about the same average score as the picture readers of Hong Kong.[9]

Contemporary whole language theory is based on the idea that the most important ingredient for many children, especially those not brought up in homes where literacy is stressed, is motivation. By putting interesting stories and good literature into the hands of children, even if they must guess at some meaning, this method aims to inspire children to love reading and to want to increase their word recognition vocabularies. A favorite technique in many schools today is "sustained silent reading," in which, at a specified time each day, all activity stops and everyone reads a book for enjoyment; every adult in the school, including janitors and other noninstructional personnel, model silent reading behavior during this dedicated time period. If today's whole language theorists are right, the damage schools now do to children's reading potential is not in failing to teach phonics but rather in spending funds on computers and software instead of well-stocked school libraries with enough (and a wide enough variety of) books to whet children's appetites for recreational reading.

Like so many of today's school controversies, the phonics squabble is a reprise of earlier conflicts in American education. In 1955 Rudolf Flesch published his best-selling *Why Johnny Can't Read*. "Ever since 1500 B.C.," he claimed, "wherever an alphabetic system of writing was used, [people] have learned to read by simply memorizing the sound of each letter in the alphabet. . . . Except twentieth century Americans. We have thrown 3500 years of civilization out the window."[10] There are no remedial reading classes "practically anywhere in the world except in the United States," said Flesch, and learning to read "never was a problem anywhere in the world until the United States switched to the present method" in about 1925.[11]

There was a kernel of truth to Flesch's diatribe about remedial reading classes being a peculiarly American development. In 1955 universal literacy was not a goal in many countries. Poor readers did not require remedial classes because they usually dropped out of school and into jobs where reading was not required. However, remedial reading had been an American school obsession for nearly half a century because compulsory education had kept children in school even when their reading progress was unsatisfactory.

The first American whole word reading primer was published in 1846. For the next century, most teaching combined whole word and phonic approaches,[12] while research increasingly recommended instruction that emphasized meaning, not sounds. In 1885, a psychologist published a study in which he concluded, after flashing words and letter combinations at laboratory subjects, that reading was learned best by recognition of whole word pictures. Another experimenter in 1898 reported similar findings.[13]

In 1893, Joseph Meyer Rice wrote *The Public School Systems of the United States*, based on observations of twelve hundred classrooms in thirty-six cities. He found that the whole word method, not phonics, was then dominant. Here is how he described a "typical" New York City classroom:

> In reading, the word method is followed. The pupils are taught to read the number of words prescribed for the grade and no more. . . . I asked the principal whether the children . . . were not able to read new words without being told what they were. She answered. . . : "How can they know what a word is when they have never seen it before? Could you recognize a thing that you had never before seen?"[14]

Rice may have overstated the extent to which phonics had been abandoned, but clearly "sounding out" new words was mostly gone from the nineteenth-century schools he observed.

In 1908, an influential textbook, Edmund Huey's *The Psychology and Pedagogy of Reading*, recommended de-emphasis of phonics and prescribed the whole language approach used in many American schools today. "Even if the child substitutes words of his own for some that are on the page, provided that those express the meaning, it is an encouraging sign that reading has been real, and recognition of details will come as it is needed," Huey wrote ninety years ago.[15]

In periods when phonetic methods prevailed, they had dubious results. Several studies published during one such interval, from 1915 to 1925, investigated why so many children failed in school. The most important cause was children not learning to read at grade level, despite drill in phonics.[16]

In 1928, the leading American reading theorist, Arthur Gates of Columbia Teachers College, published another influential text, *New Methods in Primary Reading*. Gates summarized his views by recommending that "phonetic instruction in the first grade [be greatly curtailed]; indeed it is not improbable that it should be eliminated entirely."[17]

Not that the debate was one-sided. The phonics wars proceeded as vigorously then as they do today. In 1913 a Scottish professor demonstrated that phonics was a superior method by showing that he could teach his college students to read English literature that had been rewritten using Greek letters.[18] In the year Gates published his textbook recommending no phonics, a Newark experiment tested one thousand schoolchildren and found that the better readers had learned with phonics.[19] A 1939 comparison of reading proficiency in Raleigh, where whole word and phonics instruction was combined, with that in nearby Durham, where schools relied exclusively on phonics, showed that Durham children were better readers.[20] Since the 1960s, the leading advocate of greater phonics instruction has been Jeanne Chall, whose 1967 book, *Learning to Read: The Great Debate*, concluded that a "code emphasis" (that is, phonics) "tends to produce better overall reading achievement by the beginning of the fourth grade" than what she called the "meaning emphasis" (whole word, or "look-say" method).[21] But more important, she noted that different methods may work better with different children, and that socioeconomic distinctions may bear on whether one method or another is more effective. Chall has since argued forcefully that phonics instruction may be more important for children "at risk" and less important for more academically motivated children.[22] But the dilemma is then further complicated because an emphasis on phonics may bring more "at-risk" children to basic reading competency while opening fewer doors for them to read at advanced levels.

Few school districts today, however, rely exclusively on phonics, whole word, or whole language approaches. Most good teachers combine these methods and will continue to do so. When phonics was the predominant method of instruction in the nineteenth and early twentieth centuries, teachers demanded precise recitation of practiced texts, not comprehension. As one pair of historians, Daniel and Lauren Resnick, remarked, "unless we intend to relinquish . . . comprehension as the goal. . . , there is little to go *back* to in terms of pedagogical method. . . . The old tried and true approaches, which nostalgia prompts us to believe might solve current problems, were [not] designed to achieve the literacy standard sought today."[23]

Social Promotion

Social Promotion: The Controversy

In each of his most recent State of the Union addresses (1997 and 1998), President Bill Clinton urged an end to the common practice of promoting students whose achievement is below satisfactory levels. Scores on standardized tests, he said, should "help us end social promotion . . . for no child should move from grade school to junior high or junior high to high school until he or she is ready."[24] As an alternative, the president cited a new policy in Chicago, where children who are below grade level in academic achievement must enroll in a summer remedial program before being permitted to advance. This politically fashionable pedagogy also inspired New York's Mayor Rudolph Giuliani to exclaim, in his 1998 state of the city address, that social promotion "may sound right, it may be kind, but it's cruel" because it puts off dealing with a problem that will become worse later on.[25]

According to IBM chairman Louis Gerstner, "too often schools reward students merely for showing up, not for proficiency. Because educators do not define the goals students must achieve to advance from grade to grade, students who cannot read, write or compute are promoted."[26] Teacher unions are also in agreement. In her first public speech after taking office last year, Sandra Feldman, the president of the American Federation of Teachers, lashed out at the "rampant" practice of social promotion.[27] She disclosed that a national survey of AFT members concluded that "sending students on to the next grade even though they weren't really ready" is the reason why children "graduate from high school without solid skills in reading, writing, and math." What is needed, Feldman insisted, are clear standards of performance in each subject for each grade level, and if students do not live up to those standards, they should not be promoted.

But Feldman also regarded "retention," keeping students back a grade, as unsatisfactory. Instead of these two unpalatable choices, she recommended a third way—better preschool programs, better-qualified teachers, intensive help (like the Chicago program) for children who are falling behind—so that all children can be eligible for promotion. If only they get this kind of help, she suggested, "urban kids are perfectly capable of reading well and doing well in school."

Feldman, like most critics of social promotion, assume it is a new practice, part of a broader movement to relax social standards in the latest generation. Charles Murray, whose 1984 book, *Losing Ground*, provided an intellectual justification for reversing many Great Society reforms, included social promotion as one of these misguided innovations. Because in the 1960s, Murray said, "urban schools gave up the practice of making a student repeat a grade, . . . a student who did not want to learn was much freer not to learn"; after all, the student faced "no credible sanctions for not learning."[28]

The argument is appealing. If students can move on to the next grade without learning material in their current one, they will have no incentive to study and do well. If students in a classroom are behind their peers, their teacher cannot tailor lessons to the appropriate grade level but must review and return to more elementary curricula instead. This prevents all students from learning.

But the appeal is misleading, and even Feldman's "middle ground" proposal lacks logic. While Feldman's proposed forms are desirable in their own right, they hold little hope for moving us out of the social promotion quandary. No matter what standard is set for any subject in any grade, there will be a distribution of student performance around an average. If, for example, there is a consensus that a fourth grade child "should have" read half a million words by the time he or she is ready to move on, some perfectly normal children will have read only three hundred thousand, while others will have completed their half million the previous year. Children develop unevenly, at widely different rates. An above-average child in arithmetic may be below average in reading. Some children progress faster than average in all academic subjects, while others are slower. Some slow children spurt later on, passing their peers; others always perform at normal but below-average levels.

Children differ innately, and their varied backgrounds also predispose them to varying performance levels, even if they somchow could all receive identical instruction. As noted earlier, even at the best schools, college graduates' children will likely perform, on average, better than high school dropouts' children (although some high school dropouts' children perform better than most college graduates' children). So school districts are faced with a choice: do they set standards so low that all children can meet them if special help is available? If so, the standards will present little challenge to most children and the social promotion patterns Feldman decried will prevail. Or should standards be set near the mean, on the understanding that if schools firmly establish how well fourth graders should read, many will read much better and many will read far worse? No matter how much special help is provided, and our schools could certainly offer more than they do, children performing below average will more likely be poor than rich, more likely be minority than white, more likely be immigrant than native. Communities will still face the decision whether to promote or retain these children.

Consider President Clinton's Chicago example. Summer school for children whose achievement is below grade level is an important addition to Chicago's school program. But taking into account the serious social and economic handicaps that predict relative failure for so many inner-city Chicago children, a month (or several months) of summer remediation will not bring most of them to the point where they are above average for their grade level in achievement. So Chicago will still have to decide whether to hold back these underperforming children or whether to set grade-level standards so far below average that everyone can pass. The real problem here is that those who denounce social promotion have usually failed to define what grade-level performance might be. Setting a goal for average student performance is difficult enough. Setting a minimum standard is incomparably more difficult, yet this is what the "social promotion" controversy requires.

Consider these inane instructions issued in the spring of 1998 by the California Department of Education, in the midst of a gubernatorial primary campaign in which outgoing governor Pete Wilson, as well as the leading candidates to succeed him in both parties, denounced social promotion. The department's standards defined grade-level performance as standardized test scores at the fiftieth percentile: "[we] would not want to set a standard lower than the current average performance of students in the U.S.," California declared. Then, the department proceeded to announce a goal: 90 percent of students should meet grade-level standards.[29]

But to do that, the rules of arithmetic first must be revised. The fiftieth percentile is, by definition, the score that half the nation's students exceed and half fall below. No matter how high the achievement, half the students must be below grade level, if grade level is defined as the fiftieth-percentile score.

Ninety percent of Californians can score above the nation's fiftieth percentile only if the state has a near monopoly of the best and brightest performers nationwide, while less accomplished students in other states depress national averages. Of course, other states would also prefer that 90 percent of *their* students be above average. This aspiration is out of reach for any state, much less for California, whose immigrant population arrives at school with social and economic characteristics relatively unfavorable to school success.

In Los Angeles, Superintendent Ruben Zacarias attempted a small retreat from the state's foolishness. Joining the chorus of those rejecting social promotion, he proceeded to define third grade literacy as the thirty-sixth percentile, not the fiftieth, on standardized tests. But if Zacarias wanted to abolish social promotion, did he intend that more than one-third of the district's children should repeat third grade? If, because of its more serious social and economic problems, Los Angeles's score distribution is lower than that of the nation as a whole, will the district fail the majority of third graders who test below the thirty-sixth percentile nationally? If districts elsewhere improve their performance, will Los Angeles have to hold back even more students because more of them will then fall below the thirty-sixth percentile in a national distribution?

These problems can be avoided only if retention is based not on percentile rankings but on absolute performance objectives in each subject area. Moreover, decisions will still have to be made about whether to promote students who meet the objectives in some but not all subjects. As previous chapters have shown, though, America's education policymakers, with all their sophistication, are still unable to establish valid criterion-referenced, as opposed to norm-referenced, standards. Indeed, Americans have not yet decided whether they want standards to be low (so that all children, if they are properly instructed and make a fair effort, can pass) or high (so that most children will be motivated to reach for them).

Notwithstanding the lack of clarity about these issues, if forced to choose, Feldman's teacher union members now say they would rather retain than promote. At least, they believe, this alternative will not result in watering down the curriculum for all children. But there are costs as well.

One cost is to the child kept back, whose demoralization may make further academic progress more difficult. For children whose achievement is below the mean, it is unlikely that pedagogies that failed once will now succeed if only they are repeated the following year. If these children might benefit from a different approach, they are not likely to receive it in the same classroom where they recently were unsuccessful.[30]

The effect of retention on those who do move up is equally serious. One concern with contemporary American youth is their too rapid psychosexual development. Puberty now begins earlier than it has for several hundred years. Putting fourteen-year-olds in classrooms with eleven- and twelve-year-olds will exacerbate the pressures these younger adolescents face. While grouping children by age does cause academic problems, placing children of varied ages together because of comparable academic skill is not an acceptable alternative and causes severe problems of a different nature for teachers, parents, and children alike.

Ask a seventh grade teacher, whose students are normally about twelve years old, if she wants last year's sixth graders who did not master sixth grade material in her class: the answer will be, "certainly not." This is the kind of survey Ms. Feldman's union conducted. But ask the same teacher if she wants last year's seventh graders in her class again this year because they did not master seventh grade material, and she will as adamantly object. There is no policy that can satisfy both demands—unless pupil-teacher ratios are reduced sufficiently to abolish age grading and permit each child to develop at his or her own pace. But this solution is impractically expensive. Some school systems now utilize continuous progress, grouping by multiple ages in the lower grades, where class sizes are very small. But this is no answer for the upper grades, around which most of the "social promotion" controversy swirls.

Social Promotion: The History

The dilemma of what to do with children who do not progress "normally" is not new, and it did not arise because fuzzy-headed educators were afraid to uphold standards. The dilemma is an unavoidable consequence of compulsory education. When it was considered satisfactory for children who could not keep up with their cohort to drop out, the issue of social promotion did not arise. Once they were required to remain in class, schools had to choose whether they should stay alongside their age group or their academic peers. Frequently in the twentieth century educators have felt obligated to choose the former.

But they were always aware of the conundrum. A Russell Sage Foundation report in 1908 calculated the funds being wasted in fifty-five urban school districts by teaching the same grade twice to pupils who repeated. Researcher Leonard Ayres found that 13 percent of New York's school budget was spent on students repeating a grade; the full range across cities was from only 5 percent in Newport, Rhode Island, to 30 percent in Camden.[31] The child who is held back, Ayres concluded, "humiliated by being associated with companions who are younger than he, instead of continuing . . . drops out. . . . To reduce retardation [that is, nonpromotion] would greatly enhance educational efficiency."[32]

In 1914 Stanford University researchers collected data from one hundred school districts and found wide variation. In one district, 5 percent of students were behind their age-appropriate grade; in another, 63 percent were behind.[33] The Stanford researchers also surveyed recommendations about how these numbers could be reduced. They revealed debates little different from today's. Fourteen districts proposed "more frequent promotions," eleven proposed more "individual help for slow pupils," and thirty-seven intended to implement "ungraded classes" (usually meaning more special education classes for the academically less able) or to segregate "dull or bright" students in special schools.[34]

By 1938 most school superintendents favored some form of "social promotion," according to a survey by the National Education Association.[35] In 1941 a New York Regents report concluded that "a much wiser and more profitable procedure than non-promotion is to adapt instruction to the needs of the pupils at all times, and at the end of the year to advance him to the next grade or class and there continue to adjust instruction to his needs."[36]

Philadelphia was a typical case. In the late 1930s it adopted a policy of "continuous pupil progress," but by 1946–47 the city's school board was absorbed in controversy trying to defend it.[37] The board eventually adopted a new policy after having to deny public complaints that Philadelphia schools "promoted everybody." While insisting it would continue to take social as well as academic factors into account in making promotion decisions, and that, on the whole, age is a better grouping principle than academic achievement, the board stated that it would defer to teacher recommendations in particular cases.[38]

In 1955, a *World Book Encyclopedia* research team noted that nonpromotion had steadily declined over the previous four decades. Using data assembled by the U.S. Office of Education and commercial test publishers, they calculated that the average age of U.S. students beginning the eighth grade was fourteen years in 1918, thirteen years, ten months in 1926, thirteen and seven months in 1940, and thirteen and six months in 1952.[39] Similar declines were found in each elementary grade, thanks to the phasing out of repeating students. The researchers concluded that

> the relaxing of achievement standards for promotion has given rise to greater variability in educational attainment in given grades than was formerly the case, adding to the complexity of the instructional task. . . . Since today's teacher is encouraged to concern herself with development of . . . physical, social and emotional outcomes as well as purely academic ones the advantages of this greater age-homogeneity probably outweigh the difficulties.[40]

Yet school critics have always attacked these practices. A 1950 *Life* magazine essay on schools' "grievous faults" complained that public schools

> promote all children at the end of each academic year regardless of whether their work has been good, bad or indifferent. . . . The common excuse . . . is that to withhold promotion creates in the incompetent a dangerous sense of inferiority. . . . [But] what could be better calculated to

> promote an unhealthy psychosis than to prepare a child for a world of struggle by wrapping his mind in the woolly illusion that achievement and negligence should receive the same reward?[41]

A widely reprinted 1952 speech of an Oregon school reform leader declared that the "age group promotion" system "removes the necessity of meeting definite standards and destroys incentive [because] everybody passes anyway."[42]

It is apparent that today's controversy revolves around similar irreconcilable objectives. While perhaps today's reformers will develop solutions we've not before considered, one thing is patently clear: no deterioration of school standards can be blamed on social promotion. The practice has been with us for a long, long time.

BILINGUAL EDUCATION

Bilingual Education: The Controversy

Bilingual education,* a preferred strategy for the past twenty years, aims to teach academic subjects to immigrant children in their native languages (most often Spanish) while slowly and simultaneously adding English instruction. In theory, the children do not fall behind in other subjects (math, history, science) while learning English; once fluent in English, they can make the transition to English instruction in academic subjects at the grade level of their peers. Furthermore, the theory goes, teaching immigrants in their native language shows that their family and community culture is valued and reinforces their sense of self-worth, making academic success more likely.

---

* The term "bilingual education" actually refers to all programs designed to give any support to non-English speaking children, including programs whose main focus is immersion in all English-speaking classrooms. In public debate, however, the term generally refers only to one such program, "transitional bilingual education (TBE)," in which primary (native) language instruction in academic subjects is given to non-English speakers. In this chapter, the term is used in the non-technical sense, and refers only to "TBE" programs.

In contrast, bilingual education's critics tell this story: In the early twentieth century, public schools assimilated immigrants into American culture and imparted workplace skills essential for upward mobility. Children were immersed in English instruction and, forced to "sink or swim," they swam. Today, however, separatist (usually Hispanic) community leaders and their liberal supporters, opposed to assimilation, want Spanish instruction to preserve native culture. This is especially dangerous because the proximity of Mexico, and the possibility of return to it, gives today's immigrants the option of "keeping a foot in both camps" not available to their predecessors. Today's attempts to preserve immigrants' native language and culture will not only balkanize American culture with its melting pot traditions, but also will hurt the children upon whom bilingual education is imposed because by not learning English they will be unprepared for the workplace. Bilingual education supporters may claim it aims to teach English, but high dropout rates for immigrant children and low rates of transition to full English instruction prove that, even if educators' intentions are genuine, the program is a failure.

The English First Foundation, a group lobbying to abolish bilingual education, asserts that most Americans "have ancestors who learned English the same way: in classrooms where English was the only language used for all learning activities."[43] Prominent political leaders also have inveighed against the practice. According to 1996 Republican presidential nominee Bob Dole, the teaching of English to immigrants is what we "have done . . . since our founding to speed the melting of our melting pot. . . . We must stop the practice of multilingual education as a means of instilling ethnic pride, or as a therapy for low self-esteem, or out of elitist guilt over a culture built on the traditions of the West."[44]

Adds Speaker of the House Newt Gingrich,

> If people had wanted to remain immersed in their old culture, they could have done so without coming to America. . . . Bilingualism keeps people actively tied to their old language and habits and maximizes the cost of the transition to becoming American. . . . The only viable alternative for the American underclass is American civilization. Without English as a common language, there is no such civilization.[45]

This viewpoint, like those regarding phonics and social promotion, has considerable commonsense appeal. As with so much in our education debates, though, it has little foundation in reality.

Bilingual Education: The History

During the last great wave of immigration, from 1880 to 1915, very few Americans succeeded in school, immigrants least of all. By 1930, it was still the case that half of all American fourteen- to seventeen-year-olds either did not make it to high school or dropped out before graduating.[46] Median school years completed was ten.[47]

Far from succeeding by immersing themselves in English, some immigrant groups did much worse than native-born contemporaries. The poorest performers were Italians. According to a 1911 federal immigration commission report, in Boston, Chicago, and New York, 80 percent of native white children in the seventh grade stayed in school another year, but only 58 percent of southern Italian children, 62 percent of Polish children, and 74 percent of Russian Jewish children did so.[48] A later study showed that relative immigrant failure continued into high school: in 1931, still only 11 percent of Italian-American students who entered high school graduated (compared to an estimated graduation rate of more than 40 percent for all students).[49] This was a much bigger native-immigrant gap than is evident today.

Test after test in the 1920s found that Italian immigrant students had an average IQ of about 85, compared to an average for native-born students of about 102.[50] The poor academic achievement of these Italian-Americans led to high rates of "retardation"—that is, being held back in school (this was the origin of the pejorative term, "retarded"). The federal immigration commission found that the retardation rate of children of non-English-speaking immigrants was about 60 percent higher than that of children of immigrants from English-speaking countries.[51] A survey of New York City's retarded students (liberally defined so a child had to be nine years old to be considered retarded in the first grade, ten years old in the second grade, etc.) found that 19 percent of native-born students fit this classification in 1908, compared with 36 percent of Italian-born students.[52] The challenge of educating Italian immigrant children was so severe that New York established its first special education classes to confront it. A 1921 survey disclosed that half of all (what we now call "learning-disabled") special education children in New York schools had Italian-born fathers.[53]

As these data show, some groups did better than others (as is the case today), both for cultural reasons and for reasons concerning other socioeconomic influences on student achievement. If Italian children did more poorly, Eastern European Jewish children did better. This is not surprising in light of what is now known about background characteristics that weigh powerfully on academic success. In 1910, 32 percent of southern Italian adult males in American big cities were unskilled manual laborers, but just 0.5 percent of Russian Jewish males were unskilled. Thirty-four percent of the Jews were merchants, but only 13 percent of the Italians were.[54] In New York, the average annual income of a Russian Jewish head of household in 1910 was $813; a southern Italian head of household averaged $688.[55]

But even with these relative economic advantages, the notion that Jewish immigrant children assimilated with "sink-or-swim" English education is a nostalgic and dangerous myth. In 1910, there were 191,000 Jewish children in the New York City schools; only 6,000 were in high school[56] and the overwhelming majority of these dropped out before graduating. As the Jewish historian Irving Howe put it, after reviewing New York school documents describing the difficulties of "Americanizing" immigrant children from 1910 to 1914, "to read the reports of the school superintendents is to grow impatient with later sentimentalists who would have us suppose that all or most Jewish children burned with zeal for the life of the mind."[57] There may have been relatively more of these than in other immigrant communities, Howe noted, but they were still a minority.

Immersing immigrants in an English-language school program has been effective—usually by the third generation. On the whole, immigrant children spoke their native language; the second generation (immigrants' native-born children) was bilingual but not sufficiently fluent in English to excel in school; the third generation was English-fluent and began to acquire college educations. For some groups (like Greek-Americans) the pattern more often took four generations;[58] for others (like Eastern European Jews), many in the second generation may have entered college.

This history is not a mere curiosity. Bilingual education's opponents today often claim that educators *know* how to educate immigrant children because they have done it before. If, however, Americans have never successfully educated the first or even second generation of children from peasant or unskilled immigrant families, we are dealing with an unprecedented task, and history cannot serve as a guide.

If the notion that English immersion of previous immigrant generations led to academic success is misleading, so too is the claim that bilingual education repudiates the assimilationist approach adopted by previous immigrants. Native language instruction was absent from 1920 until the mid-1960s only because a fierce anti-German and then anti-immigrant reaction after World War I succeeded in banishing it from American classrooms. Even foreign language instruction for native students was banned in most places. When Chicago's Bismarck Hotel found it necessary to rename itself "The Mark Twain," it was not surprising that bilingual education programs were also abolished.[59]

Before World War I, immigrant groups often pressed public schools to teach children in their native languages. These groups' success depended more on whether immigrant activists had political power than on a pedagogical consensus. The immigrants' objective, as today, was to preserve part of their ethnic identity in children for whom the pull of American culture seemed dangerously irresistible. In this, they were supported by many influential educators. William Harris, the St. Louis school superintendent (and later U.S. commissioner of education), argued for bilingual education in the 1870s, stating that "national memories and aspirations, family traditions, customs, and habits, moral and religious observances cannot be suddenly removed or changed without disastrously weakening the personality."[60] Harris established the first "kindergarten" in America, taught solely in German, to give immigrant students a head start in the St. Louis schools.[61]

The first bilingual public school in New York City was established in 1837, to prepare German-speaking children for eventual participation in regular English-language schools. The initial rule was that children could remain in German language instruction only for twelve months, after which they would transfer to a regular school. But the German schoolteacher resisted this rule, believing that, before transferring, the children needed more than the limited English fluency they had acquired after a year of German instruction.[62] The record is unclear about how often the teacher's resistance was successful and the rule was stretched.

Many immigrant children, not Germans alone, did not attend school at all if they were deprived of native language classes. In his

1840 address to the New York State legislature, Governor (and later Lincoln's secretary of state) William Seward explained that the importance of attracting immigrants to school, and of keeping them there, motivated his advocacy of expanded native language instruction: "I do not hesitate to recommend the establishment of schools, in which [immigrant children] may be instructed by teachers speaking the same language with themselves. . . ." Only by so doing, Seward insisted, can society "qualify . . . [them] for the high responsibilities of citizenship."[63]

Buoyed by Seward's endorsement, New York City's Italian parents demanded a native language school as well, and in 1843 the Public School Society created a committee to determine whether one should be created. The committee recommended against an Italian language school, claiming the Italian community was itself divided. "Information has been obtained," the committee averred, "that the more intelligent class of Italians do not desire such a school, and that, like most [but not, apparently, all] of the better class of Germans, they would prefer that those of their countrymen who come here with good intentions should be Americanized as speedily as possible."[64]

Bilingual education, sometimes controversial, spread nationwide. In Pennsylvania, German Lutheran churches established parochial schools when public schools would not teach in German; in 1838 Pennsylvania law converted these German schools to public schools, and then, in 1852, a state public school regulation specified that "if any considerable number of Germans desire to have their children instructed in their own language, their wishes should be gratified."[65]

In 1866, succumbing to pressure from politically powerful German immigrants, the Chicago board of education decided to set up a German-language school in each area of the city where 150 parents asked for it. By 1892 the board had hired 242 German-language teachers to instruct 35,000 German-speaking children, one-quarter of Chicago's total public school enrollment.[66] In 1870, a public school founded in Denver was taught entirely in German.[67] An 1872 Oregon law permitted German-language public schools to be established in Portland whenever 100 voters petitioned for them.[68] Maryland, Iowa, Indiana, Kentucky, Ohio, and Minnesota also had bilingual education laws, either in effect statewide or applying only to cities with large immigrant populations. In Nebraska, bilingual education enabling legislation was enacted for the benefit of German immigrant children as late as 1913.[69]

There was considerable variation in how these programs arranged what is now called "transition" to English. In St. Louis, Harris's system introduced English gradually, beginning in the first grade.[70] The 1888 report of the Missouri supervisor of public instruction stated that "in some districts the schools are taught in German for a certain number of months and then in English, while in others German is used part of the day and English the rest. Some of the teachers are barely able to speak the English language."[71] Ohio's 1870 rules provided that lower grades in German-language public schools should be bilingual (half the instructional time in grades one through four could be in German), but in grades five through eight native language instruction had to be reduced to one hour a day.[72] Baltimore permitted public schools in the upper grades to teach art and music in German only, but geography, history and science had to be in both English and German.[73] In some midwestern communities, there was resistance to any English instruction: an 1846 Wisconsin law insisted that public schools in Milwaukee must at least teach English (as a foreign language) as one academic subject.[74]

While Germans were most effective in demanding public support for native language instruction, other groups were also sometimes successful. In Texas, there were seven Czech-language schools supported by the state school fund in the late nineteenth century.[75] In California, on the other hand, a desire by the majority to segregate Chinese children seemed to play more of a role than demands by the Chinese community for separate education. San Francisco established a Chinese-language school in 1885; the city later set up segregated Indian, Mongolian, and Japanese schools.[76]

San Francisco's German, Italian, and French immigrants, on the other hand, were taught in their native languages in regular public schools.[77] Here, bilingual education was a strategy designed to lure immigrant children into public schools from parochial schools where they learned no English at all. According to San Francisco's school superintendent in 1871, only if offered native language instruction could immigrant children be brought into public schools, where, "under the care of American teachers," they could be "molded in the true form of American citizenship."[78]

Support for bilingual education was rarely unanimous or consistent. In San Francisco, election of a Republican anti-immigrant school board majority in 1873 led to the abolition of schools where French and

German had been the primary languages of instruction, and to the firing of all French- and German-speaking teachers. After protests by the immigrant community, bilingual schools were reestablished in 1874.[79] In 1877, the California legislature enacted a prohibition on bilingual education, but the governor declined to sign it.[80] William Harris's bilingual system in St. Louis was dismantled in 1888, after redistricting split the German vote and the Irish won a school board majority.[81]

In 1889, as noted in Chapter 1, Republican governor William Hoard of Wisconsin sponsored legislation to ban primary language instruction in public and private schools, claiming the support of German immigrant parents: the *Milwaukee Sentinel* published a front-page story about "a German in Sheboygan County . . . who sent his children away to school in order that they might learn English." The father, reported the *Sentinel*, complained that "in the public schools of the town, German teachers, who . . . did not know English . . . had been employed . . . [and] he felt it essential to the welfare of his children, who expected to remain citizens of this country, to know English."[82] But the newspaper and Wisconsin's Republican politicians had misjudged the immigrants' sentiments. In response to the antibilingual education law, enraged German-Americans (who had previously supported Republican candidates) mobilized to turn the statehouse over to Democrats and to convert the state's seven-to-two Republican congressional majority to a Democratic majority of eight to one. The Democrats promptly repealed the antibilingual law.[83] An almost identical series of events took place in Illinois, where formerly Republican German-American voters mobilized in East St. Louis and Chicago to elect a liberal Democrat, Peter Altgeld, governor in 1890, largely because of his bilingual school policy.[84] These upheavals in two previously safe Republican states played an important role in the election of Democrat Grover Cleveland as president in 1892.[85] Nonetheless, the controversy continued, and in 1893 the *Chicago Tribune* began a new campaign against German language instruction.[86] In a compromise later that year, German instruction was abolished in primary school but retained in the upper grades, while Chicago's mayor promised German-Americans a veto over future school board appointments to ensure that erosion of primary language instruction would not continue.[87]

But these controversies ended with World War I. Six months after the armistice, the Ohio legislature, spurred by Governor James Cox (soon to be the Democratic presidential candidate in 1920), banned all German from the state's elementary schools; the language posed "a distinct menace to Americanism," Cox insisted.[88] The *New York Times* editorialized in 1919 that although some parents "want German to be taught [because it] pleases their pride. . . it does not do their children any good."[89] Within the following year, fifteen states where native language instruction had flourished adopted laws requiring that all teaching be in English.[90] By 1923, thirty-five states had done so.[91] Only when Nebraska went so far as to ban native language instruction in parochial as well as public schools did the Supreme Court, in 1923, strike down an English-only law.[92]

During the next thirty years, bilingual instruction had mixed fortunes in places where English was not the native language. In 1950 Louisiana for the first time required English, not French, to be the language of public school instruction.[93] In the Southwest, where it had long been common to teach in Spanish, the practice continued in some places and was abolished in others. Tucson established a bilingual teaching program in 1923, and Burbank, California, started one in 1931.[94] New Mexico operated bilingual schools until the 1950s. The state even required the teaching of Spanish to English-speaking elementary schoolchildren. But in 1918 Texas made teaching in Spanish a crime; while this law was not consistently enforced (especially along the Mexican border), as recently as 1973 a Texas teacher was indicted for not teaching history in English.[95] That same year, Texas reversed itself and adopted bilingual education as its strategy.

By the time bilingual education began to reemerge in the 1970s, encouraged by a Supreme Court finding that schools without special provisions for educating minority language children were not providing equal education, the nation's memory of these precedents had been erased. Today opponents of bilingualism blithely repeat the myth that, until the recent rise of separatist minority activists and their liberal supporters, the nation had always immersed immigrant children in nothing but English and that this method had proved its effectiveness.

Bilingual Education: Mixed Evidence

This checkered history, however, does not demonstrate that bilingual education was effective, any more so than English immersion or intensive English-language instruction. Modern research on bilingual education is on the whole inconclusive. As with all education research, it is so difficult to control for complex background factors that affect academic outcomes that no single study is ultimately satisfying. Bilingual education advocates point to case studies of primary language programs in Calexico, California; Rock Point, Arizona; Santa Fe, New Mexico; New Haven, Connecticut; and elsewhere showing that children advance further in both English and other academic subjects when native language instruction is used and the transition to English is very gradual.[96] Opponents also point to case studies in Redwood City and Berkeley, California; Fairfax, Virginia; and elsewhere indicating that immersion in English, or rapid and intensive English instruction, is most effective.[97] The conflicting evidence from these case studies does not suggest that abolition of bilingual education, or even substitution of parental choice for pedagogical expertise in determining whether bilingual approaches should be used, would improve things much.

The problem is especially complex because not only economic circumstances, but also generational issues affect the achievement patterns of immigrant youth. The principal of a heavily Italian immigrant high school in New York City wrote in 1936:

> The problem of juvenile delinquency . . . baffles all the forces of organized society. . . . The highest rate of delinquency is characteristic of immigrant communities. . . . The delinquent is usually the American-born child of foreign-born parents, not the immigrant himself. Delinquency, then, is fundamentally a second generation problem. This intensifies the responsibility of the school. . . .[98]

The same is true today. The challenge now facing educators is that academic success for second-generation Hispanic and Asian children is often far below, and the dropout rate far higher than, that of children who arrive in the United States as immigrants themselves.[99] Many of these second-generation children speak English but seem fully fluent in neither English nor their home language. Some immigrant parents, frustrated that their own ambition has not been transmitted to their children, may become convinced that only English immersion will set their children straight, even as others seek bilingual solutions to prevent the corrupting influence of American culture from dampening their children's ambition.

In the absence of persuasive evidence, the issue has become politically polarized. As noted previously, in a country as large as ours, with as varied an array of experience, there is virtually no limit to the anecdotes and symbols that can be invoked as substitutes for hard data.

It is certain, however, that the American melting pot has never been endangered by pluralist efforts to preserve native languages and cultures. Bilingual instruction cannot neutralize the powerful assimilationist influences that overwhelm all children whose parents immigrate here. This is as true of Spanish-speaking children today as of turn-of-the-century immigrants.

After the most recent twenty years of bilingual education throughout America, Spanish speaking children continue to assimilate. From 1972 to 1995, despite rapidly accelerating immigration (more Hispanic youths are first-generation immigrants today than twenty years ago), the Hispanic high school completion rate has crept upward, from 66 to 70 percent.[100] Hispanic high school graduates who enrolled in college jumped from 45 to 54 percent (for non-Hispanic whites, the comparative figure is now 64 percent).[101] And the number of Hispanic high school graduates who subsequently complete four years of college climbed from 11 to 16 percent (for non-Hispanic whites, 34 percent).[102] A study of the five-county area surrounding Los Angeles, the community most affected by immigration in the nation, found that, from 1980 to 1990, the share of American-born Hispanics in professional occupations grew from 7 to 9 percent, the share in executive positions expanded from 7 to 10 percent, and the share in other administrative and technical jobs went from 24 to 26 percent.[103] In sum, 45 percent of U.S.-born Hispanics are in occupations for which good education is generally a necessity, in an area where bilingual education has been practiced consistently over the span of a generation.

Perhaps we can do better. Perhaps the United States *would* do better with less bilingual education. But perhaps not. All that can be said for sure is that the data reveal no crisis. The system of educating immigrants with which this country has been muddling through, for all its problems, does not seem to be in a state of collapse.

The best thing that could happen to the bilingual education debate, as with the controversies about phonics and social promotion, would be depoliticization. Pedagogy by soundbite is no cure for the complex social, economic, and instructional interactions that determine success for contemporary American schools.

7.

In Conclusion

American schools are not doing worse than in earlier times. Evidence seems to be that they are doing better, with the most dramatic gains coming from minority students, who have now closed some of the gap with whites in academic achievement. The teaching methods that American schools have adopted to produce these results are not simple, and they have often been applied inconsistently. But somehow they seem to have worked, if not perfectly, then far better than school critics admit. There is much that constitutes outrageously poor practice that goes on in American schools, as illustrated by a surfeit of frequently heard anecdotes. But there is also much that is effective and innovative and that has helped to produce some satisfactory, if unheralded, academic successes.

This is a big country. The measurement of any set of practices or outcomes will produce a median type as well as many cases of worse than average and better than average performance. One can, of course, attempt to reduce the number of under-performers and can implement policies to narrow the variation between below-average performers and the rest. One can attempt to shift the entire distribution of results upward, so that below-average achievers now perform at levels comparable to those of average achievers in the past. But with the multitude of social and economic influences on schools, with the diversity of population, pedagogy, and values that inspire this country's patterns of performance, one can never eliminate diverse outcomes. Certainly, we will never all be above average.

There are many aspects of the controversy surrounding our schools on which this brief volume has not dwelt. There is, for example, the furor around international test scores, which seem to show American students to be performing worse than their peers in other industrialized nations. There may be much we can learn from other nations' schools, but there also may be less to these test comparisons than meets the eye. Like the difficulties with analyzing trends in domestic test scores, there are too many confounding factors in international comparisons to make simple exam results or international rankings terribly useful. Consider the earlier discussion of why Finnish children's television watching may help them read better than American children do, or the observation that students in Iowa and North Dakota seem to have better math scores than students in Korea and Japan.

One theme of previous pages has been that social and economic characteristics interact with pedagogical practice to produce school success or failure. If this is true, however, then Americans concerned with academic achievement might get more "bang for the buck" if they concentrated more reform energies on remedying some of the scandalous socioeconomic conditions that are known to cause poor student performance. What the most productive means of attacking socioeconomic problems might be is not a subject with which this report can deal, but investigating it should be one of the highest priorities of serious school reformers.

Another idea this report has not explored is that, even if American schools are doing better than before, "better" is not good enough for a twenty-first-century economy in which workers must be much better educated. This concern is not new. School critics have always claimed, without apparent foundation, that graduates were not adequately skilled for the occupational demands of the future. Businessmen and policymakers have been making this charge with regularity since the early 1900s. Later, our terrible schools were supposed to have prepared us to lose the cold war and then the "race" for international economic competitiveness against Germany and Japan. Yet, in the past decade, the American economy's performance has been stellar in comparison to those of other industrial leaders. American workers continue to be as productive as workers anywhere, and much more productive than most, even those graduating from purportedly superior school systems.

This does not mean our schools are better than those elsewhere but only that the quality of formal education may not be the most important influence on worker productivity. Only a few years ago, most economists believed that the American economy could not tolerate unemployment of much lower than 7 percent without triggering inflation. The remaining unemployed, they thought, were so poorly educated as to be unqualified to fill newly created jobs, so more rapid economic growth would only spur competitive bidding for the services of those workers who were already employed. Yet, as the U.S. unemployment rate has drifted down to less than 4.5 percent in 1997–98, employers seem to have been able to absorb those allegedly poorly educated youths after all. The relationship between schooling and the economy is also apparently more complicated than school critics would have us believe.

The confusion here may have something to do with another abuse of statistics. A crisis atmosphere around our schools relies partly on data showing that the most rapidly growing occupations in percentage terms are those, like computer engineer, requiring more education. But a big percentage growth in occupations with small initial bases is not terribly significant. More relevant to whether America is facing a skills shortage is that the occupations most in demand, in absolute numbers, are unskilled jobs like janitors or restaurant and hotel workers. Oft-cited data about the large number of future workers expected to use computers on the job can be misleading—these data often include both retail workers who scan bar codes into computers and highly educated software designers. While the twenty-first-century economy may require more skills, the increase is not likely to be as great as people tend to believe, and what is needed may not be beyond the present capacity of our schools to provide.

This nation has more serious problems than whether it needs more skills overall. How, if opportunities for well-paid, skilled work continue to be limited, are all young people, even the least advantaged, to have a more equitable opportunity to compete for these premium slots? And if they do, how will the disappointment of previously privileged individuals forced to cede a greater share of these slots to others be accommodated? Blanket condemnation of our schools only obscures these important issues.

The message of this report—that alarms about dismal school performance are mostly unfounded—can be dangerous to the cause of legitimate school improvement, for which there remain important opportunities. Perhaps Americans can be inspired to seize these opportunities only if they believe schools are failing and in a state of crisis. It may be that unless people believe the anecdotes they hear about shameful school practices are typical, they cannot be motivated to insist on reform where it is needed.

But there is an opposite danger as well. If the hyperventilated rhetoric about school failure that has characterized popular debate for the past twenty years continues unabated, Americans may soon irrationally conclude that the public school system itself is hopeless. They may decide that attempts to fix even the worst practices cannot possibly be effective because the enormous energy devoted to school reform in the past has yielded no useful result.

Americans deserve the truth about their schools. Democratic debate is ill-served by a fable of failure. Today, cynicism is a greater danger to our public schools than complacency. Some may take the message of this book to be that we need pay no attention to our schools because they are doing just fine, thank you. But most, I hope, will conclude that there is even more reason to work to improve schools; after all, we have been pretty successful, on the whole, with the educational improvements attempted in the past.

Notes

Introduction

1. Beth Reinhard, "Cleveland: A Study in Crisis," in *Quality Counts 98: The Urban Challenge—Public Education in the 50 States* (special issue published in collaboration with the Pew Charitable Trusts), *Education Week*, January 8, 1998, p. 26.

2. Ethan Bronner, "Report Shows Urban Pupils Fall Far Short in Basic Skills," *New York Times*, January 8, 1998.

3. Reinhard, "Cleveland," p. 28.

1.

1. David Kearns, "An Education Recovery Plan for America," *Phi Delta Kappan*, April 1988, 565–70. David A. Kaplan, Pat Wingert, and Farai Chideta, "Dumber than We Thought," *Newsweek*, September 20, 1993, pp. 44–45; Louis V. Gerstner, Jr., "Don't Retreat on School Standards," *New York Times*, December 30, 1995.

2. Vance Packard, "Are We Becoming a Nation of Illiterates?" *Reader's Digest*, April 1974, pp. 81–85.

3. Charles C. Walcutt, *Tomorrow's Illiterates: The State of Reading Instruction Today* (Boston: Atlantic Monthly Press, 1961), pp. xiii–xvi, 7.

4. Jeanne Chall, *Learning to Read: The Great Debate* (New York: McGraw-Hill, 1967).

5. Jib Fowles, "Are Americans Reading Less? Or More?" *Phi Delta Kappan*, May 1993, pp. 726–30.

6. Hannah Arendt, "The Crisis in Education," *Partisan Review*, Fall 1958, pp. 493–513.

7. "Crisis in Education, Part I: Schoolboys Point Up a U.S. Weakness," *Life*, March 24, 1958, pp. 27–35.

8. "Crisis in Education, Part II: An Underdog Profession Imperils the Schools," *Life*, March 31, 1958, pp. 93–101.

9. Max Rafferty, "What's Happened to Patriotism?" *Reader's Digest*, October 1961, pp. 107–10.

10. Interview with Arthur Bestor, "What Went Wrong With U.S. Schools," *U.S. News and World Report*, January 24, 1958, pp. 68–77.

11. Rudolf Flesch, *Why Johnny Can't Read: And What You Can Do About It* (New York: Harper and Row, 1955), pp. 2–5, 132–33.

12. John Keats, "Are the Public Schools Doing Their Job?" *Saturday Evening Post*, September 21, 1957, p. 38.

13. "Failure in Los Angeles," *Time*, 1951, pp. 93–94.

14. "Crisis in Education, Part II," p. 94.

15. Evan Hunter, *The Blackboard Jungle* (New York: Simon and Schuster, 1953), pp. 83, 119.

16. Henry J. Fuller, "The Emperor's New Clothes, or Prius Dementat," *Scientific Monthly*, January 1951, pp. 32–41.

17. Albert Lynd, "Quackery in the Public Schools," *Atlantic Monthly*, March 1950, pp. 33–38.

18. Archibald W. Anderson, "The Cloak of Respectability: The Attackers and Their Methods," *Progressive Education* 29, no. 3 (January 1952): 68.

19. Benjamin Fine, *Our Children Are Cheated* (New York: Holt, 1947).

20. Fuller, "Emperor's New Clothes."

21. Cited in David L. Angus, Jeffrey E. Mirel, and Maris A. Vinovskis, "Historical Development of Age Stratification in Schooling," *Teachers College Record* 90, no. 2 (Winter 1988): 211–36.

22. Diane Ravitch and Chester E. Finn, Jr., *What Do Our 17-Year Olds Know? A Report on the First National Assessment of History and Literature* (New York: Harper and Row, 1988).

23. Benjamin Fine, "Ignorance of U.S. History Shown by College Freshmen," *New York Times*, April 4, 1943.

24. Walter Lippmann, "Education without Culture," *Commonweal*, January 17, 1941, p. 323.

25. Cited in Chall, *Learning to Read*, p. 152.

26. David C. Berliner, "Educational Reform in an Era of Disinformation," paper presented at the annual meeting of the American Association of Colleges of Teacher Education, San Antonio, Texas, February 1992, p. 54.

27. Carl F. Kaestle and Marshall S. Smith, "The Federal Role in Elementary and Secondary Education, 1940–1980," *Harvard Educational Review* 54, no. 4 (November 1982): 391.

28. Daniel P. Resnick and Lauren B. Resnick, "The Nature of Literacy: An Historical Exploration," *Harvard Educational Review* 47, no. 3 (August 1977):

370–85, citing May Ayres Burgess, *The Measurement of Silent Reading* (New York: Russell Sage Foundation, 1921), pp. 11–12.

29. Kaestle and Smith, "Federal Role in Elementary and Secondary Education," p. 393.

30. Edward L. Butterworth, "You Have to Fight for Good Schools," *Education Digest*, December 1958.

31. Samuel P. Orth, "Plain Facts about Public Schools," *Atlantic Monthly*, March 1909, p. 289.

32. Arthur G. Powell, Eleanor Farrar, and David Cohen, *The Shopping Mall High School: Winners and Losers in the Educational Marketplace* (Boston: Houghton Mifflin, 1985).

33. "The Growing Illiteracy of American Boys," *Nation*, October 15, 1896.

34. Bernard Mehl, "Educational Criticism: Past and Present," *Progressive Education* 30 (March 1953): 157.

35. Mike Rose, *Lives on the Boundary: The Struggles and Achievements of America's Underprepared* (New York: Free Press, 1989) p. 6.

36. Michael W. Kirst, "Loss of Support for Public Schools: Some Causes and Solutions," *Daedalus* 110 (Summer 1981): 59.

37. *Meyer* v. *Nebraska*, 262 U.S. 390 (1923).

38. Otis W. Caldwell and Stuart A. Courtis, *Then and Now in Education, 1845–1923* (Yonkers-on-Hudson, N.Y.: World Book Co., 1924), pp. 52, 54, 90, 125.

39. David K. Cohen and Barbara Neufeld, "The Failure of High Schools and the Progress of Education," *Daedalus* 110 (Summer 1981): 87, n. 2.

40. Even this appropriation of Rogers' humor is time-worn. It was first used in a 1958 article about the surreal character of school critics' depictions of education in the past. Butterworth, "You Have to Fight for Good Schools," p. 178.

2.

1. Thomas D. Snyder, ed., *120 Years of American Education: A Statistical Portrait*, NCES report no. 93–442 (Washington, D.C.: National Center for Education Statistics, 1993), Table 5 and Table 19.

2. Daniel P. Resnick and Lauren B. Resnick, "The Nature of Literacy: An Historical Exploration," *Harvard Educational Review* 47, no. 3 (August 1977): 382.

3. David L. Angus, Jeffrey E. Mirel, and Maris A. Vinovskis, "Historical Development of Age Stratification in Schooling," *Teachers College Record* 90, no. 2 (Winter 1988): 218–19.

4. Lester Thurow, *Head to Head: The Coming Economic Battle among Japan, Europe, and America* (New York: William Morrow and Company, 1992).

5. Ronald G. Shafer, "Washington Wire: The Wall Street Journal/NBC News Poll," *Wall Street Journal*, January 23, 1998.

6. "Manufacturers Cite Lack of Worker Skills," *Los Angeles Times*, November 15, 1997.

7. Brandon Mitchener, "Daimler's Alabama M-Class Experiment Gives a Trans-Atlantic Jolt to Stuttgart," *Wall Street Journal*, October 17, 1997.

8. Dale Hudelson, "In Washington," *Vocational Education Journal* 71 (March 1996): 12.

9. Lawrence Mishel, Jared Bernstein, and John Schmitt, *The State of Working America, 1996–97*, The Economic Policy Institute series (Armonk, N.Y.: M. E. Sharpe, 1997), Table 3.18.

10. Commission on the Skills of the American Workforce, *America's Choice: High Skills or Low Wages!* (Rochester, N.Y.: National Center on Education and the Economy, 1990), Chapter 2.

11. Lowell C. Rose, Alec M. Gallup, and Stanley M. Elam, "The Twenty-ninth Annual Phi Delta Kappa/Gallup Poll of the Public's Attitudes toward the Public Schools," *Phi Delta Kappan*, September 1997, p. 47.

12. Ibid., p. 48.

13. Ibid., p. 47.

14. This question was not asked in 1997. The last time this question was asked was in 1995. See Stanley M. Elam and Lowell C. Rose, "The Twenty-seventh Annual Phi Delta Kappa/Gallup Poll Survey of the Public's Attitudes toward the Public Schools," *Phi Delta Kappan*, September 1995, p. 43.

15. Adam Clymer, "81% in Poll Say They Would Pay Higher Taxes to Improve Nation's Schools," *New York Times*, April 11, 1983.

16. Snyder, *120 Years of American Education*, Table 4.

17. Clymer, "81% in Poll Say They Would Pay Higher Taxes."

3.

1. Otis W. Caldwell and Stuart A. Courtis, *Then and Now in Education, 1845–1923* (Yonkers: World Book Co., 1924), pp. 279–80.

2. Robert J. Mislevy, *Linking Educational Assessments: Concepts, Issues, Methods, and Prospects* (Princeton, N.J.: Policy Information Center, Educational Testing Service, December 1992), pp. 70–71.

3. Betty Hart and Todd Risley, *Meaningful Differences in the Everyday Experience of Young American Children* (Baltimore: Paul H. Brookes Publishing Co., 1995), Table 1, p. 18.

4. Terrel Bell, "Reflections One Decade After A *Nation at Risk*," *Phi Delta Kappan*, April 1993, pp. 592–97.

5. Caldwell and Courtis, *Then and Now in Education, 1845–1923*, pp. v, vi, 8, 9, 77.

6. Ibid., pp. 77–85.

7. Ibid., pp. 85–87.

8. Louise E. Raths and Philip Rothman, "Then and Now," *NEA Journal* 41, no. 4 (April 1952): 214; William S. Gray and William J. Iverson, "How Well Do Pupils Read?" in C. Winfield Scott and Clyde M. Hill, eds., *Public Education under Criticism* (Englewood Cliffs, N.J.: Prentice Hall, 1954), pp. 108–13.

9. Don C. Rogers, "Success or Failure in School," *American School Board Journal* 113, no. 4 (October 1946): 46.

10. F. H. Finch and V. W. Gillenwater, "Reading Achievement Then and Now," *Elementary School Journal* 49, no. 8 (April 1949): 446–54.

11. B. S. Bloom, "The 1955 Normative Study of the Tests of General Educational Development," *The School Review* 64, no. 3 (March 1956): 110–24.

12. Vera V. Miller, and Wendell C. Lanton, "Reading Achievement of School Children—Then and Now," *Elementary English* 33 (February 1956): 91–97.

13. Roger Farr, Leo Fay, and Harold Negley, *Then and Now: Reading Achievement in Indiana (1944–45 and 1976)* (Bloomington, Ind.: School of Education, Indiana University, 1978), pp. 7, 40, 58, 53, 61, 86, 101, 125.

14. Mable E. Boss, "Reading, Then and Now," *School and Society* 51, no. 1307 (January 13, 1940): 62–64.

15. *National Report—1997 College Bound Seniors: A Profile of SAT Program Test Takers*, College Entrance Examination Board, New York, 1997, Table 4-2, p. 7.

16. Kevin S. McGrew, "An Investigation of the Exclusion of Students with Disabilities in National Data Collection Programs," *Educational Evaluation and Policy Analysis* 15, no. 3 (Summer 1993): 339–52.

17. Mislevy, *Linking Educational Assessments*, p. 49.

18. Richard P. Phelps and Thomas M. Smith, *Education in States and Nations: Indicators Comparing U.S. States with Other Industrialized Countries in 1991*, U.S. Department of Education, National Center for Education Statistics, 1996, Figure 25.

4.

1. In practice, average scores were not very different for the few years of transition when the College Board reported both statistics. But changes in the numbers of students who take cram courses, or in the efficacy of these courses, still could affect the interpretability of SAT score trends.

2. *National Report—1997 College Bound Seniors: A Profile of SAT Program Test Takers*, College Entrance Examination Board, New York, 1997, Table 1, p. 1.

3. In 1996, the College Board changed the scale on which SAT results were reported, rendering scores reported for 1996 and after not comparable to

scores for 1995 and before. In this report, to avoid confusion, all data for 1996 and after have been converted to the original scale. Thus, scores discussed here for 1997 will be quite different from those described in newspaper accounts or in College Board publications.

4. Recentered scale scores: Verbal, 505 (standard deviation 111); Math, 511 (standard deviation 112). See ibid., Table 6, p. 9. Recentering tables were provided to the author by Nancy Ervin, program director, Educational Testing Service, Princeton, N.J., April 12, 1995.

5. Willard Wirtz, *On Further Examination: Report of the Advisory Panel on the Scholastic Aptitude Test Score Decline* (Princeton, N.J.: College Board Publications, 1997), p. 6; *National Report—1997 College Bound Seniors*, Table 6, p. 9; *National Report—College Bound Seniors: 1995 Profile of SAT and Achievement Test Takers*, College Entrance Examination Board, New York, 1995, p. 1.

6. Michael Sponhour, "Proposal Requires SAT Prerequisites: Bill Seeks to Boost State's Poor Standing," *The State* (Columbia, S.C.), January 23, 1993.

7. Howard Wainer, "Eelworms, Bullet Holes and Geraldine Ferraro: Some Problems with Statistical Adjustment and Some Solutions," *Journal of Educational Statistics* 14, no. 2 (Summer 1989): 121–40.

8. Howard Wainer, "Does Spending Money on Education Help? A Reaction to the Heritage Foundation and the Wall Street Journal," *Educational Researcher* 22, no. 9 (December 1993): 22–24.

9. Brian Powell and Lala Carr Steelman, "Bewitched, Bothered, and Bewildering: The Use and Misuse of State SAT and ACT Scores," *Harvard Educational Review* 66, no. 1 (Spring 1996): 27–59.

10. Wainer, "Does Spending Money on Education Help?"

11. Students taking the SAT in 1941 numbered 10,654. Robert J. Mislevy, *Linking Educational Assessments: Concepts, Issues, Methods, and Prospects* (Princeton, N.J.: Policy Information Center, Educational Testing Service, December 1992), p. 64. There were 2,421,000 seventeen-year-olds in the United States in 1941–42. Dividing 10,654 by 2,421,000 yields .0044, or .44 percent. Snyder, *120 Years of American Education*, Table 19. Thomas D. Snyder, *120 Years of American Education*, U.S. Department of Education, National Center for Education Statistics, Table 19.

12. There were 1,242,000 high school graduates in the United States in 1941–42. 10,654 divided by 1,242,000 equals .0086 or 0.86 percent. Snyder, *120 Years of American Education*, Table 19.

13. More precisely, 29.2 percent. There were 1,127,021 SAT test takers in 1997. *National Report—1997 College Bound Seniors*, Table 1, p. 1. About 3,859,500 Americans were seventeen-year-olds in 1997. Census estimates are from the Bureau of Census on www.census.gov., June 1, 1997.

14. *National Report—1997 College Bound Seniors*, p. 9. Scores were converted to original scale using the College Board Score Converter.

15. Recentered scores are 559 (standard deviation 103) for verbal and 571 (standard deviation 104) for math. Ibid., Table 4-2, p. 7.

16. The 1941 consumer price index equaled 14.7, using the convention that 1982–84 equals 100; *Digest of Education Statistics*, Washington, D.C., 1993, Table 40, p. 43. The December 1996 CPI-U (consumer price index for all urban consumers) equaled 158.6. *Economic Report of the President*, February 1997, Table B-58.

17. Wirtz, *On Further Examination*, p. 9.

18. Albert E. Beaton, Thomas L. Hilton, and William B. Shrader, *Changes in the Verbal Abilities of High School Seniors, College Entrants, and SAT Candidates between 1960 and 1972* (New York: College Entrance Examination Board, June 1977), p. 5.

19. Wirtz, *On Further Examination*, p. 18.

20. Beaton, Hilton, and Shrader, *Changes in the Verbal Abilities*, p. 21.

21. Wirtz, *On Further Examination*, p. 18.

22. Ibid., p. 19.

23. *National Report—College Bound Seniors, 1972–73*, College Entrance Examination Board, New York, 1972, Table 2; *National Report—College Bound Seniors, 1977*, College Entrance Examination Board, New York, 1977, Table 2.

24. Wirtz, *On Further Examination*, p. 20.

25. Ibid., p. 46.

26. Ibid., p. 25 ff.

27. *1997 Digest of Education Statistics*, National Center for Education Statistics, Washington, D.C., 1997, Table 99.

28. Beaton, Hilton, and Shrader, *Changes in the Verbal Abilities*, p. 92.

29. Ibid.

30. Paul Barton, Wirtz's assistant, whom the report described as "shar[ing] the responsibilities of the panel's chairman," recently said that he believes the entire decline in SAT scores during this period was attributable to compositional changes, not to declining school quality, although there is no way to be certain. Barton is now the director of the Educational Testing Service's Policy Information Center.

31. Diane Ravitch, "Defining Literacy Downward," *New York Times*, August 28, 1996.

32. Charles C. Carson, Robert M. Huelskamp, and Thomas D. Woodall, "Perspectives on Education in America," Systems Studies Department, Sandia National Laboratories, Albuquerque, September 24, 1991, pp. 3, 7.

33. James D. Watkins, letter to the editor, *Albuquerque Journal*, September 30, 1991.

34. The norms are established for students, not schools. Thus, if a school's sixth graders, on average, are at the fifty-fifth percentile, this does not mean necessarily that the school is at the fifty-fifth percentile for all schools.

35. In simple terms, they would do so by dropping obsolete questions from the tests, adding new ones, and then conducting a separate study to determine

how a sample of students perform on the common portions of the old and new tests. The National Assessment of Educational Progress (NAEP) invests in such studies, so historical comparisons are meaningful.

36. Cited in Anthony P. Carnevale and Ernest W. Kimmel, *A National Test: Balancing Policy and Technical Issues* (Princeton, N.J.: Educational Testing Service, 1977), p. 6.

37. John Jacob Cannell, "Nationally Normed Elementary Achievement Testing in America's Public Schools: How All 50 States Are above the National Average," *Educational Measurement: Issues and Practice* 7, no. 2 (Summer 1988): 5–8; John Jacob Cannell, *How Public Educators Cheat on Standardized Achievement Tests: The 'Lake Wobegon' Report* (Albuquerque: Friends for Education, 1989).

38. *Score Reports and Norms 1997–98*, Iowa Testing Programs, College of Education, University of Iowa, 1997; additional data supplied to the author by Professor H. D. Hoover of the College of Education, University of Iowa, January 22, 1998.

39. Mark Siebert, "Students' Test Scores Fall in Iowa," *Des Moines Register*, October 31, 1997.

40. R. B. Zajonc, "The Decline and Rise of Scholastic Aptitude Scores: A Prediction Derived from the Confluence Model," *American Psychologist* 41, no. 8 (August 1986): 862–63.

41. Daniel Koretz, *Trends in Educational Achievement* (Washington, D.C.: Congressional Budget Office, 1986), p. 36.

42. *NAEP 1994 Trends in Academic Progress*, NCES 97–095, National Center for Education Statistics, Washington, D.C., 1996, p. 53; *NAEP 1996 Trends in Academic Progress*, NCES 97–985, National Center for Education Statistics, Washington, D.C., 1997, Figure 3.3, p. 61.

43. Except that there was an insignificant drop of one point from the high point in 1994 to 1996 in the average score of the highest and middle two quartiles.

44. Except that in 1996, the highest quartile's average score remained unchanged since 1992, and the lowest quartile had had no change from its high point in 1994. See *NAEP 1996 Trends in Academic Progress*, Figure 3.3, p. 61.

45. *Educational Achievement Standards: NAGB's Approach Yields Misleading Interpretations*, GAO/PEMD-93-12, U.S. General Accounting Office, 1993, p. 14.

46. June Kronholz, "Opponents Sharpen Pencils over National Testing Plan," *Wall Street Journal*, September 8, 1997.

47. *Setting Performance Standards for Student Achievement: A Report of the National Academy of Education Panel on the Evaluation of the NAEP Trial State Assessments—An Evaluation of the 1992 Achievement Levels* (Stanford, Calif.: National Academy of Education, 1993), pp. 91–92.

48. Estimated from the following: The figure of 187,397 math scores higher than 600 comes from *National Report—1992 College Bound Seniors: 1992*

Profile of SAT and Achievement Test Takers, College Entrance Examination Board, New York, 1992, p. 9. There were 2,341,000 public high school seniors in 1992; refer to, *Digest of Education Statistics, 1997*, National Center for Education Statistics, Washington, D.C., 1997, Table 43. Private secondary enrollment as a percentage of total secondary enrollment in 1992 was 9.9 percent; see *Digest of Education Statistics, 1997*, Table 3.

49. Albert E. Beaton, et al., *Mathematics Achievement in the Middle School Years: IEA's Third International Mathematics and Science Study* (Chestnut Hill, Mass.: TIMSS International Study Center, 1996); Albert E. Beaton et al., *Science Achievement in the Middle School Years: IEA's Third International Mathematics and Science Study* (Chestnut Hill, Mass.: TIMSS International Study Center, 1996).

50. Warwick B. Elley, *How in the World Do Students Read?* (Hamburg: International Association for the Evaluation of Educational Achievement, 1992), p. 14.

51. *Educational Achievement Standards*, p. 12.

52. Ibid., pp. 31–32.

53. *Setting Performance Standards for Student Achievement*, pp. xxii, 148.

54. Ibid., p. xxiv.

55. *Educational Achievement Standards*, p. 57.

56. A. D. deGroot, "The Effects of War upon the Intelligence of Youth," *Journal of Abnormal and Social Psychology* 43, no. 3 (July 1948): 311–17.

57. A. D. deGroot, "War and the Intelligence of Youth," *Journal of Abnormal and Social Psychology* 46, no. 4 (1951): 596–97.

58. Wendy M. Williams and Stephen J. Ceci, "Schooling, Intelligence and Income," *American Psychologist* 52, no. 10 (October 1997): 1051–58.

59. James R. Flynn, "The Mean IQ of Americans: Massive Gains, 1932 to 1978," *Psychological Bulletin* 95, no. 1 (1984): 29–51.

60. James R. Flynn, "Massive IQ Gains in 14 Nations: What IQ Tests Really Measure," *Psychological Bulletin* 101, no. 2 (1987): 171–91.

5.

1. Charles E. Silberman, "A Devastating Report on U.S. Education," *Fortune*, August 1967, p. 181.

2. *National Report on College Bound Seniors 1975–76*, College Entrance Examination Board, New York, 1976, p. 7.

3. Recentered scale scores: Verbal, 505 (standard deviation 111) = 428; Math, 511 (standard deviation 112) = 487. *National Report—1997 College Bound Seniors: A Profile of SAT Program Test Takers*, College Entrance Examination Board, New York, 1997, Table 6, p. 9. Recentering tables were

provided to the author by Nancy Ervin, program director, Educational Testing Service, Princeton, N.J., April 12, 1995.

4. *National Report on College Bound Seniors 1975–76*, Table 2, p. 12.

5. *National Report—College Bound Seniors: 1991 Profile of SAT and Achievement Test Takers*, College Board, New York, 1991, calculated from Table B, p. v.

6. *National Report—1997 College Bound Seniors*, Table 4-1, p. 6, and Table 1, page 1.

7. Recentered scale scores: Verbal, 526 (standard deviation 101) = 449; Math, 526 (standard deviation 103) = 504. It is difficult to be precise about the proportion of white test-takers in 1976 because so many SAT test takers declined to fill out the Student Descriptive Questionnaire (SDQ) in that year. Those who identified themselves as white on the SDQ were 67 percent of all test takers, but 85 percent of all those who responded to the race/ethnic question on the SDQ. If one assumes that nonwhites were less likely to respond to the question than whites, and that more nonwhites were likely to describe themselves as white than vice versa, it is likely that the true figure was closer to 85 percent than to 67 percent. By 1997, relatively more test takers answered the race/ethnic question on the SDQ, allowing for more certainty about the accuracy of recent numbers. In 1997, those who identified themselves as white on the SDQ were 62 percent of all test takers and 68 percent of those who answered the race/ethnic question.

8. Blacks who identified themselves as such were 6.5 percent of all test takers and 8.2 percent of all self-identifiers. *National Report on College Bound Seniors 1975–76*, Table 2, p. 12.

9. *National Report—College Bound Seniors: 1991 Profile of SAT and Achievement Test Takers*, calculated from Table B, page v.

10. *National Report—1997 College Bound Seniors*, Table 4–1, p. 6, and Table 1, p. 1. Students who identified themselves as black represented 9.8 percent of all test takers, 10.8 percent of self-identifiers.

11. Recentered scale scores, Verbal, 434 (standard deviation 101) = 356; Math, 423 (standard deviation 97) = 389.

12. The number of black seventeen-year-olds, July 1, 1976: 592,000; number of black seventeen-year-olds, June 1, 1997: 610,000. U.S. Department of Commerce, Bureau of the Census, Statistical Information Office, Population Division.

13. *Digest of Education Statistics 1996*, National Center for Education Statistics, 1996, Table 8. This assumes that the typical seventeen-year-old in 1976 and the typical seventeen-year-old in 1997 were both born to parents who were between twenty-five and twenty-nine years old. In April 1960, 38.6 percent of blacks and those from other nonwhite races between the ages of twenty-five and twenty-nine years old had completed four years of high school;

in March 1980, 77 percent had done so. In April 1960, 5.4 percent of blacks and those from other nonwhite races between the ages of twenty-five and twenty-nine years old had completed four years of college; in March 1980, 15.2 percent had done so.

14. The most recent data in *Digest of Education Statistics* are from March 1995. The precise figures are 84.6 percent high school graduates and 19.4 percent college graduates. These data are probably slightly overstated because they are for "blacks and other races," and the numbers for blacks are probably lower than the numbers for "other races." On the other hand, the numbers are probably slightly understated because the educational attainment of parents of black high school and college graduates is probably higher than that of parents from the same cohort whose children did not graduate.

15. *National Report on College Bound Seniors 1975–76*, Table 2, p. 12; there were 12,221 Mexican-American test takers in 1976. *National Report—1997 College Bound Seniors*, Table 4-1, p. 6; there were 36,689 Mexican-American test takers in 1997.

16. *National Report—College Bound Seniors, 1991 Profile of SAT and Achievement Test Takers*, calculated from Table B, p. v.

17. Recentered scale scores: Verbal, 451 (standard deviation 102) = 373; Math, 458 (standard deviation 99) = 426.

18. The 1980 Census listed 982,479 Mexican-origin fifteen- to nineteen-year-olds; U.S. Department of Commerce, Bureau of the Census, Table 48, pp. 1–51. The 1990 Census listed 1,289,615 Mexican-origin fifteen- to nineteen-year-olds; U.S. Department of Commerce, Bureau of the Census, Statistical Information Office, Population Division, Table 114, p. 123.

19. The 1980 Census showed 227,013 Puerto Rican-origin fifteen- to nineteen-year-olds; U.S. Department of Commerce, Bureau of the Census, Population Division, Statistical Information Office, Table 48, pp. 1–51. The 1990 Census indicated 238,497 Puerto Rican-origin fifteen- to nineteen-year-olds; U.S. Department of Commerce, Bureau of the Census, Statistical Information Office, Population Division, Table 114, p. 123. The data reported here are for the Puerto Rican cohort living on the mainland. It is possible that some Puerto Rican test takers lived in Puerto Rico, but inasmuch as the SAT is given only in English, the numbers of such students are not likely to be sufficiently large to affect the point made here.

20. Recentered scale scores: Verbal, 454 (standard deviation 104) = 376; Math, 447 (standard deviation 103) = 416.

21. *NAEP 1996 Trends in Academic Progress*, NCES 97–985, National Center for Education Statistics, Washington, D.C., 1997, Figure 3.4, p. 63.

22. Ibid., Figure 3.3, p. 63.

23. *NAEP 1996 Trends in Academic Progress*, Figure 3.3, p. 64. *NAEP 1992 Trends in Academic Progress*, Washington, D.C., 1994. Figure 4.2, p. 80.

24. *NAEP 1996 Trends in Academic Progress*, Figure 3.3, p. 64.

25. *The Condition of Education 1997*, NCES 97–388, Office of Educational Research and Improvement, Indicator 18, p. 86.

26. Author's estimate based on data from ibid. and from *The Condition of Education 1996*, NCES 96–304, National Center for Education Statistics, Washington, D.C., Indicator 15, Table 15–3, p. 224.

27. Author's estimate based on data from *The Condition of Education 1995*, NCES 95-273, National Center for Educational Statistics, Washington, D.C., 1995, indicator 13, Table 13–3, p. 205, and *Condition of Education 1997*.

28. *NAEP 1996 Trends in Academic Progress*, Figure 5.4, p. 113. Raw scores come from *Condition of Education 1997*, Indicator 15, p. 80. Gap calculations come from *Report in Brief: NAEP 1996 Trends in Academic Progress*, NCES 97–986, National Center for Education Statistics, Washington, D.C., 1997.

29. *NAEP 1996 Trends in Academic Progress*, Figure 5.4, p. 113.

30. David W. Grissmer, *Education Productivity* (Washington, D.C.: Council for Educational Development and Research, 1997), p. 22.

31. David W. Grissmer, et al., *Student Achievement and the Changing American Family* (Santa Monica, Calif.: RAND, 1994), p. xix.

32. Ibid., pp. 16–17.

33. Ibid., p. 95.

34. Ibid.

35. Ulric Neisser, et al., "Intelligence: Knowns and Unknowns," *American Psychologist* 51, no. 2 (1996): 77–101.

36. Lynn Olson and Caroline Hendrie, "Pathways to Progress," *Quality Counts 98: The Urban Challenge—Public Education in the 50 States* (special issue published in collaboration with the Pew Charitable Trusts), *Education Week*, January 8, 1998, p. 34.

37. Kati Haycock, et al., *Education Watch: The 1996 Education Trust State and National Data Book* (Washington, D.C.: Education Trust, 1996), pp. 12–13.

6.

1. Christina Duff, "How Whole Language Became a Hot Potato in and out of Academia," *The Wall Street Journal*, October 30, 1996.

2. Sheryl WuDunn, "Calligraphy Slips in Japan, Pushed by Computer," *New York Times*, December 18, 1996.

3. Robert Leetsma et al., *Japanese Education Today* (Washington, D.C.: U.S. Government Printing Office, 1987), pp. 29–30.

4. Warwick B. Elley, *How in the World Do Students Read?* (Hamburg: International Association for the Evaluation of Educational Achievement, 1992), pp. 52–53.

5. This does not suggest that American children could improve their reading by watching television. For American children, reading scores on the international test were lower the more television they watched. Our television programs obviously do not require facility with decoding subtitles. Ibid., Figures 7.6 and 7.7, p. 72.

6. Rudolf Flesch, *Why Johnny Can't Read: And What You Can Do About It* (New York: Harper and Row, 1995), p. 81.

7. Jeanne Chall, "*Learning to Read: The Great Debate* 20 Years Later: A Response to 'Debunking the Great Phonics Myths,'" *Phi Delta Kappan* 70 (March 1989): 522–23.

8. Elley, *How in the World Do Students Read?* Table 4.1, p.24.

9. Stephen D. Krashen, *Every Person a Reader: An Alternative to the California Task Force Report on Reading* (Culver City, Calif.: Language Education Associates, 1996).

10. Flesch, *Why Johnny Can't Read*, pp. 4–5.

11. Ibid., p. 2.

12. Ibid., pp. 46ff.

13. Ibid., p. 50.

14. J. M. Rice, *The Public School System of the United States* (New York: Century Co., 1893), p. 38.

15. Cited in Flesch, *Why Johnny Can't Read*, p. 52.

16. Gates, Arthur I., "A Review of *Tomorrow's Illiterates* by Charles C. Walcutt and *What Ivan Knows that Johnny Doesn't* by Arthur S. Trace, Jr." (no publishing data), 1961.

17. Cited in Flesch, *Why Johnny Can't Read*, p. 55.

18. Ibid., p. 61.

19. Ibid., p. 62.

20. Ibid., p. 66; cited in Chall, "*Learning to Read: The Great Debate* 20 Years Later," p. 533.

21. Jeanne Chall, *Learning to Read: The Great Debate* (New York: McGraw-Hill, 1967), p. 137.

22. Chall, "*Learning to Read: The Great Debate* 20 Years Later."

23. Daniel P. Resnick and Lauren B. Resnick, "The Nature of Literacy: An Historical Exploration," *Harvard Educational Review* 47 no. 3 (August 1977): 385. Emphasis in original.

24. Quoted in Arthur Reynolds, Judy Temple, and Ann McCoy, "Grade Retention Doesn't Work," *Education Week*, September 17, 1997.

25. Dan Barry, "Giuliani Calls for Changes in New York School System," *New York Times*, January 15, 1998.

26. Louis V. Gerstner, Jr., "Don't Retreat on School Standards," *New York Times*, December 30, 1995.

27. *Passing on Failure*, report, American Federation of Teachers, Washington, D.C., 1997; Sandra Feldman, "Passing on Failure: The Problem of

Social Promotion in Schools," Address to National Press Club, September 9, 1997.

28. Charles Murray, *Losing Ground: American Social Policy 1950–1980* (New York: Basic Books, 1984), p. 173–74.

29. To district and county superintendents, et al. from Ruth Ann McKenna, chief deputy superintendent for educational policy, curriculum and department management, California Department of Education (Memorandum, April 15, 1998).

30. As an education analyst, I have a selfish professional reason for being suspicious of increased retention policies: they make it even more difficult to trust data on student achievement. An easy way to make it appear that student achievement is improving is to prevent the slowest learners from advancing a grade; that grade's test scores will suddenly shoot up. The effect of the retained students on the scores of the younger cohort in whose grade they are now placed will vary and be hard to isolate. They could depress those scores or raise them, all without any real change in pedagogical effectiveness. And these effects will vary from district to district, depending on their retention policies. Indeed, to the extent that retention policies now differ, this becomes another difficulty in interpreting data on student achievement.

31. Leonard P. Ayres, "The Money Cost of the Repeater," *The Psychological Clinic* 3, no. 2 (April 15, 1909): 56.

32. Ibid. pp. 51, 57.

33. Hilda Volkmor and Isabel Noble, "Retardation as Indicated by One Hundred City School Reports," *The Psychological Clinic* 8, no. 3 (May 15, 1914): Table III, p. 78.

34. Ibid., p. 81.

35. David L. Angus, Jeffrey E. Mirel, and Maris A. Vinovskis, "Historical Development of Age Stratification in Schooling," *Teachers College Record* 90, no. 2 (Winter 1988): 228–29.

36. Lloyd H. Elliott, "Promote All—In the Public Schools?" *Educational Forum* 13, no. 1, Part I (November 1948): 69–72.

37. Angus, Mirel, and Vinovskis, "Historical Development of Age Stratification in Schooling," p. 229.

38. "Philadelphia Schools Solve the Promotion Problem," *Elementary School Journal* 48 (June 1948): 532; Angus, Mirel, and Vinovskis, "Historical Development of Age Stratification in Schooling," p. 230.

39. Roger T. Lennon and Blythe C. Mitchell, "Trends in Age-Grade Relationships: A Thirty-five Year Review," *School and Society*, October 15, 1955, p. 124.

40. Ibid., p. 125.

41. Bernard Iddings Bell, "Our Schools: Their Four Grievous Faults," in C. Winfield Scott and Clyde M. Hill, eds., *Public Education under Criticism* (Englewood Cliffs, N.J.: Prentice-Hall, 1954), reprinted from *Life*, October 16, 1950.

42. Mrs. W. T. Wood, "The Teaching of Fundamentals," in Scott and Hill, *Public Education under Criticism*, reprinted from *Vital Speeches of the Day*, March 1952.

43. From English First website <http://www.englishfirst.org.>

44. Mark Pitsch, "Dole Takes Aim at 'Elitist' History Standards," *Education Week*, September 13, 1995, p. 18.

45. Newt Gingrich, *To Renew America* (New York: HarperCollins, 1995), pp. 161–62.

46. *Digest of Education Statistics*, National Center for Education Statistics, Washington, D.C., 1996, Table 55. 1929 30, enrollment in grades nine to twelve in public and private schools equaled 50.7 percent of the total population fourteen to seventeen years of age.

47. Thomas D. Snyder, ed., *120 Years of American Education: A Statistical Portrait* (Washington, D.C.: U.S. Department of Education, National Center for Education Statistics, 1993), Table 5. In 1940, the median figure for years of school completed by twenty-five- to twenty-nine-year-olds was 10.3.

48. Michael R. Olneck and Marvin Lazerson, "The School Achievement of Immigrant Children: 1900–1930," *History of Education Quarterly*, Winter 1974: Table 5, p. 459.

49. Seymour B. Sarason and John Doris, *Educational Handicap, Public Policy and Social History: A Broadened Perspective on Mental Retardation* (New York: Free Press, 1979), pp. 350–51.

50. Ibid., pp. 155–56, 343.

51. David K. Cohen, "Immigrants and the Schools," *Review of Educational Research* 40, no. 1 (1970): 13–27.

52. Sarason and Doris, *Educational Handicap*, p. 340.

53. Ibid., p. 342.

54. Olneck and Lazerson, "School Achievement of Immigrant Children," Table 11, p. 469.

55. Ibid., Table 12, p. 470.

56. Irving Howe, *World of Our Fathers* (New York: Simon and Schuster, 1983), p. 277. Consider this back-of-the-envelope calculation. If there had been an even distribution of ages represented in the youth population, and all Jewish youths completed the eighth grade, there would have been 185,000 Jewish students in grades one to eight, or approximately 23,000 students per grade. Had these students all continued to graduate, there should have been about 93,000 Jewish high school students. That there were only 6,000 suggests a dropout rate of 85 percent. Of course, the distribution of age cohorts was not even; because immigration had just peaked at this time, it is possible that the youth population would reach a maximum a few years later. But even positing a disproportionate number of young children in the New York Jewish population of 1919, the dropout rate would have been enormous.

57. Ibid., p. 278.

58. Rosalie Pedalino Porter, *Forked Tongue: The Politics of Bilingual Education* (New York: Basic Books, 1990), p. 169.
59. Mary J. Herrick, *The Chicago Schools: A Social and Political History* (Beverly Hills, Calif.: Sage Publications, 1971), p. 61.
60. Diego Castellanos, *The Best of Two Worlds: Bilingual-Bicultural Education in the United States*, CN 500 (Trenton: New Jersey State Department of Education, 1983), p. 23.
61. Ibid., pp. 24–25.
62. Sarason and Doris, *Educational Handicap*, pp. 180–81.
63. Ibid., p. 194.
64. Ibid., p. 181.
65. Heinz Kloss, *The American Bilingual Tradition* (Rowley, Mass.: Newbury House, 1977), pp. 149–50.
66. Herrick, *Chicago Schools*, p. 61.
67. Kloss, *American Bilingual Tradition*, p. 180.
68. Ibid., p. 86.
69. Castellanos, *Best of Two Worlds*, p. 19.
70. Ibid., pp. 24–25.
71. Kloss, *American Bilingual Tradition*, p. 69.
72. Ibid., pp. 158–59.
73. Ibid., p. 190.
74. Ibid., p. 86.
75. Ibid., pp. 177–78.
76. Ibid., p. 184.
77. Castellanos, *Best of Two Worlds*, p. 23.
78. Paul E. Peterson, *The Politics of School Reform, 1870–1940* (Chicago: University of Chicago Press, 1985), p. 55.
79. Ibid.
80. Ibid., p. 56.
81. Castellanos, *Best of Two Worlds*, p. 25; James Crawford, *Bilingual Education: History, Politics, Theory, and Practice* (Trenton: Crane Publishing Company, 1989), p. 22.
82. "The School Question," *Milwaukee Sentinel*, November 27, 1889.
83. William F. Whyte, "The Bennett Law Campaign in Wisconsin," *Wisconsin Magazine of History*, June 1927, pp. 363–90.
84. Herrick, *Chicago Schools*, p. 61; Peterson, *Politics of School Reform*, p. 10.
85. Kloss, *American Bilingual Tradition*, p. 89.
86. Bernard Mehl, "Educational Criticism: Past and Present," *Progressive Education* 30 (March 1953): 154.
87. Peterson, *Politics of School Reform*, p. 58.
88. Crawford, *Bilingual Education*, p. 23.
89. Ibid.
90. Ibid., p. 24.

91. David Tyack, "Constructing Difference: Historical Reflections on Schooling and Social Diversity," *Teachers College Record* 95, no. 1 (Fall 1993): 15.

92. *Meyer* v. *Nebraska*, 262 U.S. 390 (1923).

93. Castellanos, *Best of Two Worlds*, p. 49.

94. Ibid., p. 43.

95. James Crawford, *Hold Your Tongue: The Politics of English Only* (Reading, Mass.: Addison-Wesley, 1992), p. 72; Crawford, *Bilingual Education*, p. 26.

96. Rudolph Troike, "Research Evidence for the Effectiveness of Bilingual Education," *NABE Journal* 3, no. 1 (1978): 13–21; *The Bilingual Education Handbook: Designing Instruction for LEP Students* (Sacramento: California Department of Education, 1990), p. 13.

97. Troike, "Research Evidence for the Effectiveness of Bilingual Education," p. 3; Iris Rotberg, "Some Legal and Research Considerations in Establishing Federal Bilingual Policy in Bilingual Education," *Harvard Educational Review* 52, no. 2 (May 1982): 158–59; Porter, *Forked Tongue*, p. 141.

98. Leonard Covello, "A High School and Its Immigrant Community: A Challenge and an Opportunity," *Journal of Educational Sociology* 9, no. 6 (February 1936): 334.

99. Ruben G. Rumbaut, "The New Californians: Research Findings on the Educational Progress of Immigrant Children," in Ruben Rumbaut and Wayne A. Cornelius, eds., *California's Immigrant Children: Theory, Research, and Implications for Educational Policy* (La Jolla, Calif.: Center for U.S.-Mexican Studies, University of California, San Diego, 1995).

100. *Dropout Rates in the United States 1995*, NCES 97–473, National Center for Education Statistics, Washington, D.C., 1997, Table A–37, p. 89.

101. *The Condition of Education 1997*, NCES 97–388, National Center for Education Statistics, Washington, D.C., 1997, Indicator 8, p. 62.

102. Ibid., Indicator 22, p. 94.

103. Gregory Rodriguez, "The Emerging Latino Middle Class," Pepperdine University, 1996, Figure 22, p. 14.

INDEX

About the Author

Richard Rothstein is a research associate of the Economic Policy Institute, where he specializes in trade, labor, and educational policy. He is also an adjunct professor of public policy at Occidental College in Los Angeles, a founding member of the Pacific Council on International Policy, and a contributing editor of *The American Prospect.*